T0342916

More Praise for
THE ITALIAN SUMMER KITCHEN

"Skimming through these pages is as refreshing as jumping in the Mediterranean on a hot summer's day. . . . Each recipe is worthy of a perfect summer meal."
　　　—JANIE HIBLER, James Beard Award–winning author of
　　　　　　　Dungeness Crabs and Blackberry Cobblers

"A delightful and nuanced interpretation of Italian summer. . . . *The Italian Summer Kitchen* is like a big sunny warm embrace from Italy. Filled with charming illustrations and informative sidebars, it's a must-have for anybody passionate about cooking good food and Italy."
　　　—SARA JENKINS, chef/owner, Nina June restaurant

"In this enchantingly illustrated cookbook, Cathy Whims transports you to summertime in Italy, with regional recipes incorporating the glorious summer produce that abounds. . . . Make room on your cookbook shelf for an Italian cookbook unlike any other."
　　　—DIANE MORGAN, author of *Pizza*

continued

THE ITALIAN
SUMMER KITCHEN

THE ITALIAN SUMMER KITCHEN

Timeless Recipes for La Dolce Vita

CATHY WHIMS

Illustrations by Kate Lewis

Countryman Press

An Imprint of W. W. Norton & Company
Independent Publishers Since 1923

For information about permission to reproduce selections from this book, write to
Permissions, Countryman Press, 500 Fifth Avenue, New York, NY 10110

For information about special discounts for bulk purchases, please contact
W. W. Norton Special Sales at specialsales@wwnorton.com or 800-233-4830

Manufacturing by Elcograf
Book design by Allison Chi
Production manager: Devon Zahn

Countryman Press
www.countrymanpress.com

An imprint of W. W. Norton & Company, Inc.
500 Fifth Avenue, New York, NY 10110
www.wwnorton.com

978-1-68268-918-9

1 0 9 8 7 6 5 4 3 2 1

FROM CATHY: *For my mother, Ann Virginia Thomas Whims,
who taught me to appreciate the pleasures of the table
and all the joy and togetherness they bring.*

FROM KATE: *To Linn and Michelle—from our Nettelhorst
days until now—thank you for always cheering me on.*

CONTENTS

INTRODUCTION

I COULD SAY this book was born from spending languorous summers in Italy twirling forkfuls of spaghettini and clams, with my toes in the sand. Or from the hours I spent learning how to turn gnarly potatoes into cloudlike gnocchi in the kitchen with Marcella Hazan herself. I could even say it was inspired by my preoccupation with young, tender zucchini and their jubilant, sunshiny blossoms. Each of these statements would be true. But they wouldn't explain the "why" of this book. For that, I have to start at the very beginning.

I was lucky enough to grow up with a mother who loved to cook and did so supremely well. She was an early devotee of Julia Child, and our family meals in Chapel Hill, North Carolina, were delicious reflections of her passion for good food. With that kind of upbringing, it would have been a surprise if I didn't end up just as passionate about food, and after college, it felt so natural to carve out a career as a chef.

I moved to Portland, Oregon, in 1979, and five years later, I got my dream job working at Genoa, one of the city's most venerable fine dining restaurants. Like most chefs at that time, I believed that the only way to elevate my food was to make it as complicated as possible, as if the only way to be taken seriously as a chef was to prove yourself by how many components you could pack into a dish. This was my mindset as I worked my way up from line cook at Genoa, to its executive chef, and eventually co-owner. Often, the menus I created weren't even centered on Italian food, even though the restaurant shared its name with the birthplace of pesto. It was, first and foremost, a special occasion restaurant—fine dining with a Mediterranean accent—and, at the time, fine dining meant fussy.

It didn't help that, at least in the beginning, I was cooking Italian food despite never having been to Italy. But then I finally made it there in my mid-thirties, fell in love with everything about the country, the cuisine, and the culture, and began traveling there semi-regularly. It soon dawned on me that the kind of food I was cooking at Genoa was not what I was eating on my travels, which was simple, stripped down, and ingredient driven. That's when I realized I had some serious unlearning to do.

I had to learn to take things away instead of adding them. Instead of dreaming up complicated sauces, I schooled myself on the difference between anchovies from the Adriatic Sea versus the Mediterranean. Instead of brainstorming more garnishes, I painstakingly chose the perfect variety of bean for our minestrone soup. I developed close relationships with local farmers and learned all I could about the heirloom varieties they were bringing to market.

When I opened Nostrana in 2005, it gave me the platform to focus on making regional

Italian food the Italian way—with the emphasis on the ingredients—and it was an immediate success. Two decades later, it's still one of the city's most beloved restaurants.

In many ways, cooking at Nostrana also brought me back to my roots. I had turned my back on the food I grew up with because it wasn't fancy enough. But as I gained a deeper appreciation for ingredients, I realized that Italian food has a lot in common with the food I had eaten in the South. Think polenta versus grits, prosciutto versus country ham—they're just two sides of the same coin. Both cuisines have strong agrarian cultures built around the seasons, local ingredients, and an unfussy celebration of place. It's no wonder I fell so hard for Italian food. It resonates with me at a cellular level.

At Nostrana, even though our menu is unequivocally Italian, that doesn't mean we're chained to tradition. In the Italian spirit of cooking with what's growing close at hand, we let our Pacific Northwest ingredients guide our creativity.

And that leads me back to the inspiration behind this book. It's not about cheffy, complicated twists from a 40-year restaurant veteran. It could be, but it's not. It could be about slavish re-creations of traditional dishes from a longtime student of Italian cuisine. But it's not. Instead, it's about learning how to recognize and truly appreciate ingredients in their prime and cook with them in a way that brings out their very best. And there's no better way to showcase this philosophy than through Italian food and no better season than summer.

These pages all take their inspiration from that "la dolce vita" vibe that characterizes the spirit of Italy in the summer. There's a distinct slowing down and appreciation of the pleasures of the table. People spend more time eating alfresco and put aside their everyday routines to spend August at the beach or in the mountains. There's almost a sense of romanticism to how Italians approach summer, which is why each recipe in this book is illustrated with dreamy watercolor illustrations from the immensely talented Kate Lewis. Inspired by my favorite memories and ingredients, they let you fill in the blanks with your own daydream of summer in Italy better than any photograph could.

In true taking-it-easy fashion, you won't need a ton of time, money, or fancy equipment to execute these recipes well, just a commitment to finding the best ingredients. Otherwise, what's the point? The Pappa al Pomodoro (page 52) made with ordinary supermarket tomatoes won't taste anything like one made from homegrown or farmers' market tomatoes.

If there's one theme to this book, it's that delicious food doesn't have to be complicated—something Italians know very, very well. And if there's one goal, it's that it inspires you to slow down, cook a little, and enjoy the flavors of the season, no matter where summer takes you.

Salute!

Cathrine A Whims

PANTRY

TO AVOID CONFUSION, it's worth noting that for the recipes in this book, butter is unsalted, eggs are large, Parmesan is Parmigiano-Reggiano aged at least one year and grated fresh and finely on a Microplane, sea salt for cooking is fine, and sea salt for finishing is flaky. Black pepper is always freshly ground, and herbs measured in cups are loosely packed.

Most of the recipes in this book are built on familiar, easy-to-find ingredients. That being said, I definitely prefer some brands or versions of those ingredients more than others, and they're usually imported from Italy. When I can't find my favorites locally, Gustiamo's online store is my go-to. Here's a peek into my pantry:

Anchovies (Salt Packed versus Oil Packed)

I used to bring back jars of salt-cured anchovies when I visited the tiny Amalfi fishing village of Cetara, the Italian anchovy capital, wrapping them fastidiously in plastic and praying they didn't break open in my suitcase. Now, I order Nettuno brand salt-cured anchovies in jars from Gustiamo.

To clean salt-cured anchovies, use your fingers to remove the desired number of fillets from the jar (a tool might slice or crush them). Redistribute the layer of salt over the top of the jar before covering and refrigerating. Scrape the excess salt off the fillets and rinse each in cold water. Split each little fish in two, starting on the belly side and gently sliding your thumb along the edge, inserting it until you can separate the two halves and pull them apart. The bones will stay on one half, so pinch them in the middle and pull them off. Wipe or pull off any bits of fin or entrails, rinse again gently, and then soak in cool water on a shallow plate or bowl to remove a bit more of the salt, about 10 minutes. Taste, and if they're still aggressively salty, soak in fresh cool water for another several minutes. When the salt level is still assertive but pleasant, pat dry with paper towels and proceed with your dish. The prepared anchovies will be good for up to four days.

Spanish Cantabrian anchovy fillets packed in oil are amazing as well and don't need any preparation. Just drain off the oil and proceed. Cantabrian anchovies come from the Atlantic Ocean, which is colder and deeper than the Mediterranean Sea and produces better-tasting fish. Bahia de la Concha is my favorite brand. Rizzoli brand anchovy fillets in a spicy sauce, which I discovered thanks to cookbook author Domenica Marchetti, are best in pasta sauces or on bruschetta.

Whether you use salt-packed or oil-packed, these are salt-cured anchovies that shouldn't be confused with white anchovies (boquerones), which are mildly pickled.

Balsamic Vinegar

The world of balsamic vinegar can be confusing. If you want the best, your first clue will be the price. Expect to spend $30 to $60 or more per *ounce*, depending on how long it was aged. Your second clue is the label "traditional balsamic vinegar." But the most important indicator is the Aceto Balsamico Tradizionale di Modena (or di Reggio Emilia) DOP certification. Only vinegars made in Reggio Emilia and Modena in the traditional method can earn it. If you invest in a bottle, treat it like the ultra-luxe garnish it is—never heat it or waste a drop.

The best Italian mass-produced balsamics, the kind perfect for whisking into dressings or reducing to a glaze on the stove, should have the designation "Balsamic Vinegar of Modena IGP." This means it was made and processed in Modena with traditional grape varieties, though they may have been grown outside the region. Check the ingredients list to make sure you get one without any thickening agents or colorants.

"Condimento" balsamic is an unregulated term, which means you can find it slapped on labels for lovely high-quality vinegars as well as garbage. The best Italian condimento vinegars are made in the traditional way but didn't get the DOP certification, either because they weren't produced under the supervision of the Consorzio di Balsamico Condimento, weren't aged as long, or weren't made in Modena or Reggio Emilia. They're still expensive but cheaper than traditional balsamic. There are some lovely American-made condimento balsamics, too. To ensure a top-notch bottle, look at the ingredients list: grape must should be the first and ideally only ingredient, not wine vinegar.

Bottarga

This is a salted and dried sac of fish roe, usually mullet (which is cheaper) or tuna (which is more expensive and fishier). Buy it whole, not pregrated, and slice or grate it into finished dishes that need a little savory-salty oomph.

Carnaroli Rice

I prefer Carnaroli rice for things like risotto and Rice and Bean Salad (page 36) because it has a little more structure and resists getting mushy. Acquerello is considered one of the best brands in Italy and is my personal favorite. It's aged at least one year (their ultrapremium option is aged seven years), which allows it to absorb more liquid as it cooks, resulting in bigger, more flavorful grains.

Garlic (Summer versus Winter)

We often don't think of garlic as a seasonal vegetable because it stores so well that we have ready access to it year-round, but it helps to keep garlic's growing season in mind when deciding how much to use in a recipe.

Garlic begins sprouting in the spring, which is when you can find scallion-like green garlic bulbs at farmers' markets. Garlic in this form has a mild flavor and you can use the whole thing, green tops and all. By summer, the tops have turned brown and died off, and farmers will start harvesting the young, fresh, tender bulbs. Summer garlic is definitely less pungent than bulbs that have dried and gone into storage for the winter. So, you may want to use more garlic in summer and dial it back when making the same dish in winter.

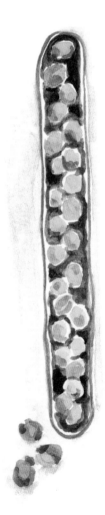

Once peeled, garlic takes on unpleasant, acrid notes, so I don't recommend buying bags of already-peeled cloves or jars of crushed garlic. It's well worth the extra couple of minutes to peel and mince your own.

Honey (Mild)

I love using honey instead of sugar because it adds floral complexity, especially when I'm making agrodolce (sour-sweet) dishes that employ just a bit of sweetness to offset the piccante (spicy) flavors. Be sure to use a mild honey (anything but chestnut, really) so that the flavors don't clash, and choose raw honey, which isn't heated and processed.

Mayonnaise

I always prefer to make my own mayonnaise or aioli (essentially garlic mayonnaise) because the flavor and texture are so much more fresh and luscious than anything store-bought. But there are, of course, times when the need for speed prevails and I reach for Duke's mayonnaise. A southern brand that's increasingly common outside the region, it has a soft, silky texture and savory flavor that's the closest to homemade.

Olives (Italian)

Italy grows hundreds of varieties of olives, and they're all worth exploring. Green olives are simply unripe and usually milder and more herbal in flavor, and are cured in a salt brine. Black olives have been allowed to ripen to maturity and have more complex fruity or tannic notes. They can be brine cured or salt cured, which produces wrinkly, chewy texture and more intense flavor. Some olives are tiny;

some are huge and perfect for stuffing with cheese or roasted peppers. Some olives are sold only green or only black; others you can find in both states.

Any olive you like can have a place on a meat and cheese board (especially big and buttery Castelvetrano), but when it comes to cooking, some varieties are better than others. I prefer Gaeta or Taggiasca olives for most dishes because they both are flavorful but not polarizing, and easy to find.

Gaeta olives are small oval olives from the coastal town of Gaeta, between Rome and Naples. They're most often sold ripened into a dark purple hue and either salt cured and wrinkly, or plump and brine cured, with a meaty texture and tart flavor similar to Kalamata olives but a little more complex.

Taggiasca olives are sweeter and smaller and hail from Liguria on the Italian Riviera. If you've had a Niçoise olive, then you know what they taste like because they're the same variety. But Taggiasca olives are usually cured in an herbal brine that adds to their flavor.

Cerignola olives are big, sweet, meaty, and almost always green. They're ideal for raw preparations, such as meat and cheese boards or salads, especially when you don't want an olive with too much tart or tannic bite.

Olive Oil (Extra-Virgin)

It's ideal to keep several kinds of extra-virgin olive oil on hand. You'll need an affordable but high-quality general-purpose oil for cooking. At the restaurant, we use Séka Hills Arbequina estate-grown olive oil from California. For sauces and for drizzling, where the flavor of the olive oil really makes an impact, try to use a mild oil, such as Taggiasca, for delicate dishes; use a peppery oil, such as those produced from Tuscany or Umbria, for heartier dishes. Frescobaldi's Laudemio, Tenuta di Capezzana, and Pianogrillo from Sicily are some of my favorites.

The Italian olive harvest generally occurs in November and hits shelves soon after, so learn how to read an olive oil label for its vintage. You should only pay top dollar for oils no more than a year old. If you can't find the harvest date, check the expiration, which is usually set two years from the date it was bottled. Any oil in your pantry that is three years old is only good for deep-frying.

Keep in mind: The younger the oil, the stronger the flavor, as it contains the highest amount of polyphenols, which keep the oil bright, intense, and fruity. These mellow as the oil ages throughout the year. In Italy, the rule of thumb is to dress your food with this year's oil and use last year's for cooking.

Oregano (Sicilian)

Sicilian-grown oregano is renowned for its intense aroma with complex notes of mint and marjoram, flowers, and spices. The good stuff is hand harvested and slowly dried to preserve the essential oils. It's often sold in branches, but I prefer the convenience of dried leaves packed in jars. For those recipes when dried oregano works better than fresh, I use only Sicilian oregano because it's far more interesting and pungent than anything else. If you don't have it, you may need to use larger amounts of dried oregano when making these recipes.

Pasta (Dried)

These days, a really dizzying amount of imported dried pasta brands is available in the States. That's a good problem to have, though it makes it harder to pick one. Benedetto Cavalieri, Faella, Martelli, and Rustichella d'Abruzzo are some of my favorite brands. They're extruded using bronze dies, which gives them a rough texture perfect for sauces to cling to, and they're slowly air dried to preserve their wheaty flavor. When shopping for pasta, these are the qualities to look out for. When the usual supermarket brands are the only option, my pick is DeCecco. As for fresh pasta, I don't recommend buying it. It's so easy to make yourself (see page 183) and will always taste better.

Pine Nuts

Pine nuts, aka pignoli, are actually seeds from the pine cones of certain varieties of pine trees that grow all over the world. However, true Italian pine nuts come from stone pines growing along the west coast of Italy. Unlike nut trees that produce a harvest every year, stone pine cones can take several years to mature and produce seeds, and the harvest is labor intensive, to boot. Hence the high price. But their tender texture and buttery flavor, especially when lightly toasted, make pine nuts a favorite addition to everything from pastas to desserts (and Genovese pesto wouldn't be the same without them).

Nowadays, you can find pine nuts at any grocery store, but chances are they're not from the stone pine. One way to tell is the size: seeds from the stone pine are long and slender. Another telltale sign is the price. Expect to pay $5 to $10 an ounce. If you're paying far less, they're likely a mix of species from all over the world. There's nothing wrong with that, but there's some evidence to suggest pine nuts from at least one variety of tree can sometimes cause people to experience an unpleasant lingering metallic taste 12 or so hours after eating them. Called "pine mouth" or "pine nut syndrome," the effect can linger for days or weeks, making everything you eat taste metallic. Thankfully, it goes away on its own.

Research as to why this happens is all over the place. Some studies suggest the culprit is a specific variety of pine tree that typically grows in a specific area of China, but since pine nuts can come from over 200 varieties of trees and are often combined when packaged for sale, the jury is still out. More recent studies suggest it tends to happen to "supertasters," those people who carry a gene for enhanced bitter receptors. If you ask me, there's no reason to avoid pine nuts, but there's a very good reason to spring for the good stuff. Seek out packages that clearly label the origins. Peeled almonds and walnuts make a great alternative, but make sure they're sweet and fresh, not old and bitter.

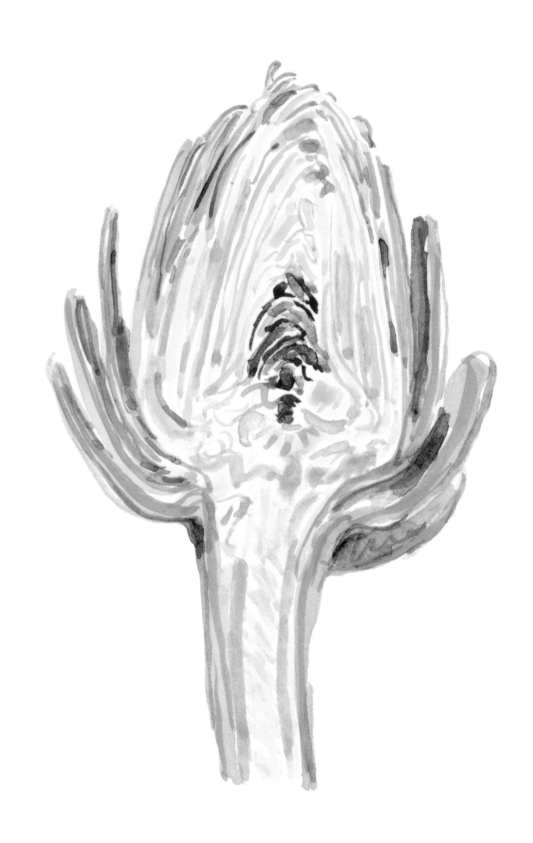

Sea Salt (Fine, Flaky, and Coarse)

I prefer using sea salt over regular table salt or kosher salt because it's less processed and contains trace minerals. Sea salt comes in fine, flaky, and coarse textures. Flaky sea salt is usually pretty expensive because it's hand harvested to preserve the texture and often comes from special harvesting areas. I reserve this for finishing dishes. Fine is cheaper and dissolves quickly, so it's my go-to for cooking. If you want to use coarse sea salt, it's best for salting pasta water (use a light hand). Most of my ingredient listings for salt do not specify a quantity because the amount of salt you need to enhance the flavors in your food really depends on your personal palate.

Semolina/Semola Rimacinata Flour

Italian pasta is made with semolina flour, which is ground from a flavorful species of hard wheat called durum wheat. Semolina has a texture similar to cornmeal, which is a bit too coarse for fresh pasta (although good for dusting a pizza peel), so I use semola rimacinata, which is finely ground semolina. It's also great for pizza, breads, and other baked goods.

Tuna (Canned)

Olive oil–packed tuna has a rich, moist texture that's far superior to the dry shreds of water-packed tuna. And if you want the absolute best, look for ventresca, which means "belly," as this will be even fattier and therefore more luscious and flavorful. Tuna labeled "Bonito del Norte" from Spain is fabulous, Ortiz is a good brand that's widely available, and I also love La Brújula brand. Although you can use the oil the tuna was canned in, I usually drain it off because I prefer the flavor of fresh oil.

Tomatoes (Canned)

When using canned tomatoes, the gold standard is imported San Marzanos with the DOP symbol on the label. DOP means "Denominazione d'Origine Protetta," a prized status only conferred on a select few traditional Italian ingredients, such as true San Marzanos grown in the Sarno Valley in the shadow of Mount Vesuvius. When you see this on the label, you know it's the real deal. But if you want to save a few bucks, non-DOP tomatoes can be delicious, too. Keep in mind that whole tomatoes are usually higher quality than chopped or otherwise processed, so it's better to buy whole and cut them up yourself. In general, Italian imports are preferable because they will be canned in rich tomatoey juices, rather than water, and preserved with salt rather than calcium chloride, which can make the tomatoes too firm to break down properly. One of my favorite imported brands is Gustarosso. For domestic, I love Bianco Di Napoli, cofounded by famed pizza chef Chris Bianco and made with California-grown tomatoes canned in the Italian style.

TOOLS

Equipment

Charcoal grill
Colander
Fine-mesh strainer
Food mill
Food processor and/or blender or
    immersion blender
Kitchen scale
Mixing bowls
Pasta machine
Stand mixer with whisk, paddle,
    meat grinder, and sausage
    stuffer attachments

Pots and Pans

Nonreactive (e.g., stainless steel) 4-quart
    heavy-bottomed saucepan
Medium (8-inch) and large (12-inch)
    sauté pans
10-inch nonstick skillet
Large pot
Large Dutch oven
Roasting pan
Rimmed half-sheet baking pans
    (13 by 18 inches)
Baking dishes: 9 by 13 inches and
    8 by 8 inches

Utensils

Fish spatula
Deep-frying thermometer
Instant-read meat thermometer
Liquid and dry measuring cups
Meat pounder
Microplane grater
Mortar and pestle
Slotted spoon
Tongs

Supplies

Cheesecloth
Kitchen twine
Parchment paper

Ombrellone Pâté

MAKES 1¾ CUPS

I have a friend in Italy who rents an umbrella at a lido in the seaside town of Capalbio for the whole summer, not unlike how Americans might have summer long pool memberships so they can take a dip anytime the fancy strikes. One day, I joined her at the beach and came out of the water ravenous after swimming. She handed me a piece of bread topped with this murky-brown tuna-caper spread, and although it wasn't attractive, I gratefully tucked in. Under that bright umbrella, with the salt from the sea still on my lips, it was like being handed a taste of the Mediterranean Sea I had just been swimming in. Magical! For me, this bright, briny, and incredibly versatile pâté will forever be synonymous with lazy summer days spent under a beach umbrella, hence the name.

Three 4-ounce cans oil-packed tuna, drained

8 oil-packed anchovy fillets

3 tablespoons salted capers, rinsed, soaked in water for 10 minutes, and drained

6 tablespoons extra-virgin olive oil

3 tablespoons red wine vinegar

¼ teaspoon grated lemon zest

1 tablespoon freshly squeezed lemon juice

¼ cup minced fresh flat-leaf parsley leaves

Sea salt and freshly ground black pepper

Combine the tuna, anchovy fillets, capers, oil, vinegar, and lemon zest and juice in a food processor. Pulse until combined for a more rustic texture, or process until smooth. Add the parsley and pulse until combined. Taste and add more lemon juice, plus salt and pepper, if desired.

Serve the pâté with crackers, crostini (see page 4), or Bruschetta (page 6), crudités, or as spread for light sandwiches.

Tramezzini Ideas

Spread the pâté on white sandwich bread and top with thinly sliced radishes and cucumbers. Or top with a few slices of Marinated Zucchini (page 11). Cut off the crusts, quarter into triangles, and serve.

Tuscan-Style Chicken Liver Crostini

SERVES 6 AS AN APPETIZER

Sit down at a Tuscan trattoria and it's not uncommon for this rustic pâté to arrive at your table unbidden. It's so traditional it borders on integral—and with good reason. When sautéed with anchovies and capers, and doused in a splash of nutty-sweet vin santo, the lowly chicken liver transforms into a deeply savory and utterly luscious spread for crisp crostini. It's also great on grilled Bruschetta (page 6) cut into bite-size pieces. This is an easy appetizer that feels somehow super deluxe, and it's fabulous with a refreshing, brightly acidic white wine on a warm summer evening (or, really, anytime of year). Think sauvignon blanc or, better yet, go fully Tuscan with a bottle of Vernaccia di San Gimignano or Verdicchio di Matelica from the Marche region right next door.

8 ounces chicken livers

1 tablespoon unsalted butter

⅓ cup plus 1 tablespoon extra-virgin olive oil

½ small white onion, chopped finely

6 fresh sage leaves, chopped finely

1 bay leaf

¼ cup vin santo or dry Marsala

3 oil-packed anchovy fillets, chopped finely

1 tablespoon capers, drained, rinsed, and chopped

Flaky sea salt and freshly ground black pepper

½ baguette, sliced ⅓ inch thick

Rinse the chicken livers and cut away any sinew or yellow spots. Heat the butter and 1 tablespoon of the olive oil in a large skillet over medium heat until sizzling. Add the onion and sauté until softened, about 7 minutes.

Add the chicken livers, sage, and bay leaf, then sauté until the livers are opaque and slightly browned, about 5 minutes. Pour in the vin santo and simmer until evaporated. Continue to cook the livers until they are just barely cooked inside and lightly browned on the outside.

Use a slotted spoon to transfer the livers to a cutting board. Chop into ½-inch pieces. Return the livers to the pan and add the chopped anchovies and capers. Cook over low heat, stirring to break the mixture into a crumble, until the liver pieces are just barely pink, about 2 minutes. Season with salt and pepper to taste.

To make the crostini, heat the remaining ⅓ cup of olive oil in another large skillet over medium-high heat. Add the bread slices and fry both sides until golden, 3 to 4 minutes per side.

Spread the chicken liver mixture on the crostini and serve while still warm.

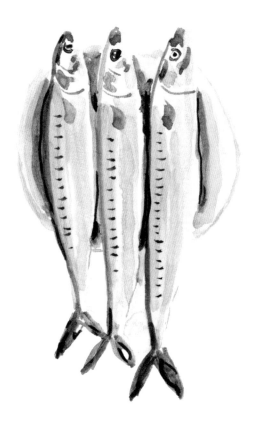

Bruschetta con Salsa di Pomodoro
WITH VARIATIONS
SERVES 4

Thick and chewy slices of rustic artisan bread are satisfying on their own, but when you add a kiss of char and a hint of garlic, they're a reason for living. They're also a fabulous vehicle for all kinds of toppings. Diced tomatoes are the classic choice here, but don't stop there. Try adding a smear of ricotta and a drizzle of good balsamic. Or top the toasts with an entirely different spread. Even Eggplant Caponata (page 50) would be a great choice. If you have any leftover bruschetta, cube it and add it to panzanella, Insalata Nostrana (page 30), or Rice and Bean Salad (page 36).

SALSA DI POMODORO

2 medium or 1 large heirloom tomato

1 garlic clove, minced

6 large fresh basil leaves, torn into small pieces

¼ cup plus 1 tablespoon extra-virgin olive oil

Sea salt and freshly ground black pepper

BRUSCHETTA

4 slices country bread, cut in half

1 garlic clove, cut in half

Extra-virgin olive oil for drizzling

Flaky sea salt

TO MAKE THE SALSA DI POMODORO

Core the tomato(es) and chop finely. Place in a small bowl along with the garlic, basil, and olive oil. Season with salt and pepper to taste. Allow to marinate for 10 minutes before serving.

TO MAKE THE BRUSCHETTA

Grill, broil, or toast the bread slices on both sides until lightly charred. While the bread is still warm, rub the cut side of the garlic clove on one side. (Resist the urge to rub all over. A couple of swipes will suffice.) Drizzle the bread generously with olive oil. Sprinkle with salt. Spoon the salsa on the bread slices and serve.

Variations

- Top with Marinated Zucchini (page 11) instead of salsa di pomodoro.
- Spread with Homemade Ricotta (page 189) before topping with the salsa di pomodoro or with Marinated Zucchini (see page 11). Or simply drizzle the ricotta with grassy olive oil and sprinkle with pepper and fresh herbs.
- Spread with Ombrellone Pâté (page 2) and top with watercress.
- Top with Salsa Piccante (page 171) or Eggplant Caponata (page 50).
- Layer with Taleggio and sliced Marinated Mushrooms (page 10). Lightly broil until melty.

How to Assemble a Fabulous Salumi Platter

Charcuterie boards are for the French. In Italy, it's il tagliere, and it's a win-win for the person who puts it together as much as for those who get to enjoy it. That's because a well-thought-out platter of cured meats (aka salumi) and cheeses is less about cooking than it is about shopping, plus it indulges our basic human need for snacking. Still, there's an art to assembling a platter that's truly party worthy, and it's all about variety—in shapes, colors, textures, and especially flavors. Here are the 10 general rules of engagement:

1. Good prosciutto is the cornerstone of il tagliere. It's nonnegotiable. And there are far more varieties of prosciutto in Italy than we see in the States. The most common here is prosciutto di Parma, sweet and salty, from the Emilia-Romagna region. Prosciutto San Daniele, from the Friuli-Venezia Giulia region in the far north, is made on a smaller scale, more intense in flavor, and more expensive. Then there's prosciutto Toscano, which is rubbed with pepper and wild juniper for a slightly spicy flavor. Why not get all three and taste the differences?

2. Prosciutto is a kind of whole-muscle salami, but it's not the only one. Try contrasting it with slices of coppa (usually spicy or just well spiced) and speck (like smoked prosciutto).

3. Add a few contrasting sweet and spicy coarse-ground salami, such as fennel-y finocchio, salame piccante, or soppressata. There are hundreds of kinds of salami, which are salted and seasoned blends of meat and fat that are dry cured. For maximum interest, visit a good deli or specialty market and aim for at least three in a variety of flavors, shapes, and sizes. You'll even find variations in the size of the pockets of fat in the meat.

4. If you're ordering the meats sliced, don't opt for ultrathin because the slices will stick to each other and tear. Think postcard thickness, not tissue paper.

5. Contrast your assortment of hard salami with softer cooked varieties, such as luscious mortadella and rich, spreadable 'nduja (pronounced en-doo-yuh).

6. You could have a salumi-only platter, but it's nice to have some cheeses in the mix. Again, variety is the name of the game. Include a soft, spreadable cheese, such as Robiola or ricotta, which you can flavor with herbs and whip into a fluffy dip. Add wedges of a semi-firm cheese, such as fresh pecorino or Taleggio. Then, graduate into the hard cheeses, such as Parmigiano-Reggiano and aged pecorino. If you like blue cheese, Gorgonzola is a quick way to punch things up. Don't feel obligated to opt solely for imports. Many artisan cheesemakers in the United States make wonderful cheeses in the Italian style.

7. Both salumi and cheeses will taste more flavorful if not consumed ice cold from the fridge. Let the meat sit out for a few minutes before serving to take the chill off so the flavors can bloom, but don't wait so long that they become melty and greasy.

8. To add a personal touch and an accent note of bright piquancy, incorporate a homemade preserve from your kitchen, such as the Marinated Mushrooms (page 10), Marinated Zucchini (page 11), Cantaloupe Confettura (page 191), or Rosé and Champagne Vinegar Cherries (page 192).

9. Don't forget the carbs. You'll need some simple crackers, grissini or other breadsticks, Bruschetta (page 6), Focaccia (page 90), or just a crusty bread like ciabatta or a baguette as vehicles for those meats and cheeses.

10. Fill in the platter with nuts and fresh or dried fruits for added pops of color and to encourage more grazing.

Marinated Mushrooms

SERVES 8 TO 12 AS AN APPETIZER

We typically focus on wild mushrooms at Nostrana—porcini, shiitake, morels, chanterelles, and other delights that grow in our local forests and come to us by way of dedicated foragers. With ready access to these exciting varieties, it's easy to forget about the basic button, but I'll be forever grateful to chef Klaus Monberg for showing me how this quotidian supermarket mushroom can be just as satisfying when treated right.

Monberg, a Danish-born Oregon transplant trained by famed French chef Roger Vergé, taught me that the trick to making button mushrooms as flavorful as their more exotic cousins is to get rid of their excess moisture, thereby concentrating the earthy umami flavors hidden within. A quick boil in salted water helps the mushrooms release some of their liquid and allows the marinade flavors to soak in. In just a few days, they're transformed into tender and intensely flavorful little nuggets perfect for garnishing cured meats on a charcuterie platter, tossing in tender lettuce salads, tucking into tramezzini, or, as Monberg used to do at his exquisite little Oregon Coast restaurant in the '90s, serving them alongside pâté en croûte. Marinating is one case where using a fancier mushroom would be a waste.

2½ pounds button mushrooms, ends
trimmed

2 tablespoons sea salt

⅓ cup extra-virgin olive oil

3 tablespoons white wine vinegar

6 to 8 garlic cloves, peeled and crushed

½ yellow onion, peeled and grated into a
bowl to catch the juice

Rinse the mushrooms in a large colander under cold running water. Transfer to a large pot. Add the salt and just enough cold water to cover. Bring to a boil over high heat, stirring occasionally, as the mushrooms will bob about and need to cook consistently. Once the water boils, remove from the heat and drain the mushrooms in a colander.

While the mushrooms come to a boil, mix together the oil, vinegar, garlic, onion, and onion juice in a large bowl. Add the mushrooms while they're still hot. Allow to cool, cover, and refrigerate for 3 to 4 days and season with salt to taste before serving. Mushrooms in this marinade will keep, refrigerated, for up to 2 weeks.

Marinated Zucchini with Chickpea Fritters
(ZUCCHINI ALLA SCAPECE CON PANELLE)
SERVES 6, WITH 24 FRITTERS

Bright with vinegar and fresh herbs, this is a refreshing way to use young, early-season zucchini (forget the big, spongy specimens), and it's perfect for piling onto Bruschetta (page 6) or adding to a platter of antipasti with other fresh or roasted vegetables. But I think I love it best of all paired with golden panelle (chickpea fritters). In Livorno, you'll often find marinated eggplant and crispy slabs of panelle tucked into soft rolls to make the classic cinque e cinque sandwich, but I love zucchini scapece so much I use that and skip the bread so it can really shine. Frying the zucchini slices removes some of the moisture so they stay firm while marinating, and the oil they soak up in the process tames the vinegar bite. The method works wonderfully well for eggplant, too. The golden fritters, gorgeously crispy outside and wonderfully luscious inside, are naturally gluten-free and are ideal accompaniments to predinner bubbles and spritzes. Use good olive oil in the batter, but for frying this is a good time to use older vintages of olive oil that have been hanging out in the back of your cabinet or opt for vegetable oil. This recipe makes a big batch of marinated zucchini, and you'll be happy it does. It keeps for a week and is so delicious to have on hand.

ZUCCHINI ALLA SCAPECE

2 pounds small, early-summer zucchini

1 tablespoon flaky sea salt, plus more to taste

⅓ cup white wine vinegar or red wine vinegar

⅓ cup finely chopped fresh mint leaves

4 garlic cloves, peeled and sliced thinly

Extra-virgin olive oil for frying

PANELLE

¼ cup plus 1 tablespoon flavorful extra-virgin olive oil, plus more for oiling pan

1 small onion, diced finely (about ¾ cup)

3 garlic cloves, minced (about 2 tablespoons)

1 teaspoon minced fresh rosemary

3 cups water

1½ cups chickpea flour

⅛ teaspoon sea salt, plus more to taste

Extra-virgin olive oil for frying

continues

TO MAKE THE ZUCCHINI ALLA SCAPECE

Slice the zucchini into ¼-inch-thick rounds. Toss with the salt in a colander until well distributed. Let drain for 1 to 2 hours. Rinse briefly and dry well on paper towels.

Combine the vinegar, mint, and garlic in a small bowl. Let the garlic marinate while you fry the zucchini.

Set a cooling rack inside a baking sheet, lay a few sheets of paper towels on top, and place it near the stove. Heat ½ inch of olive oil in a 10- to 12-inch, straight-sided sauté pan over medium heat until shimmering (it should be about 350°F). Working in batches, fry the zucchini until deep golden brown on both sides, about 10 minutes per side. Transfer to the paper towel–lined rack as you go. Place the fried zucchini in a large baking dish and add the vinegar mixture. Season with salt, if necessary, and toss well. Use right away or allow to marinate for 1 hour.

TO MAKE THE PANELLE

Oil a 9-by-13-inch baking dish.

Heat 1 tablespoon of the olive oil in a medium, heavy-bottomed pot over medium heat. Add the onion, garlic, and rosemary. Sauté until soft but not browned, about 7 minutes.

Add the remaining ¼ cup of olive oil and the water, increase the heat to high, and bring the mixture to a boil. Slowly whisk in the chickpea flour, stirring constantly to prevent lumps. Continue to whisk until the mixture is smooth and well combined. Add the salt, lower the heat to low, and gently simmer, whisking occasionally, for 5 minutes.

Pour the mixture into the prepared pan; it should be about ¼ inch thick. Remove from the heat and allow it to cool to room temperature, then refrigerate for at least 1 hour.

Remove the panelle from the dish and slice it into 2-inch squares.

Line a baking sheet with paper towels to drain the panelle after frying and set near the stove. Heat 2 inches of oil in a large pot or deep fryer to approximately 350°F. Working in batches to avoid overcrowding the pot and lowering the temperature of the oil, carefully fry the panelle until golden brown and slightly puffed, about 5 minutes.

Use a slotted spoon to transfer the fried panelle to the paper towel–lined baking sheet. Sprinkle lightly with sea salt.

TO ASSEMBLE

Cut the panelle fritters horizontally to create a little pocket. Tuck a few slices of the marinated zucchini inside and serve. Refrigerate any leftover zucchini for up to 1 week and bring back to room temperature before serving.

Aperitivo Time

Aperitivo is not just a predinner drink in Italy; it's a tradition, one that started in the north and spread throughout the country because it's just such a wonderful idea. In the evening hours, you meet up with friends in a caffè or bar, order a drink, and get served an assortment of salty little snacks to go with it, things like tiny tramezzini or crostini with toppings, olives, potato chips, or crispy little fritters. Usually, these are simple, refreshing cocktails and spritzes, built with a backbone of bitter amari, to help you unwind after a long day and at the same time prime your appetite for the dinner hours to come. And, usually, the snacks are just nibbles, not meant to replace dinner but to fuel your second wind (although some places now offer apericena—a portmanteau of "aperitivo" and "cena," or dinner).

The recipes in this chapter are ideal for creating your own Italian-style aperitivo hour. Of course, you'll need the perfect, icy cold, bracingly bitter cocktail to go with it. Here are four favorites.

A Quintessential Negroni

SERVES 1

At Nostrana, we're known for our rotating cast of creative spins on this classic Italian drink. We've had a Negroni of the Month program for years, with guest bartenders from around the country chiming in with their riffs. And our industry party, the Negroni Social, spawned a nationwide event called Negroni Week. This drink is the one that started it all, and more than a decade later, it's still the most popular cocktail on our menu.

1 ounce Campari

1 ounce Bombay Dry Gin

1 ounce Cinzano Sweet Vermouth

Orange peel for garnish

Stir together all the ingredients in a mixing glass with ice until chilled. Strain into a 12-ounce rocks glass with a large ice cube or into a chilled coupe. Garnish with orange peel.

Negroni Sbagliato

SERVES 1

The Negroni is a heavy hitter, but the Negroni Sbagliato is more spritzy in style. Sbagliato means "wrong" or "mistaken," and the cocktail was so named in the late 1980s, when a bartender in Milan accidentally used sparkling wine instead of gin when making a Negroni. This fizzy take has far less alcohol, making it ideal for sweltering days when you need a lighter form of refreshment.

1 ounce Cinzano Sweet Vermouth

1 ounce Carpano Botanic Bitter
   or Campari

Prosecco

Orange twist for garnish

Fill a collins glass with ice. Pour in the vermouth and Carpano. Top with Prosecco and garnish with an orange twist.

Petali di Rosa

SERVES 1

With rose-steeped liqueur, herbal gin, and citrusy amaro, this refreshing spritz from Nostrana bartender Russell Smith calls to mind sunny summer days in a rose garden. The Elena Gin is made by my friends who used to own Vietti winery in Piedmont. It's juniper-forward in the London dry style, with a host of regional ingredients, including almonds, wild thyme and mint, coriander, and black elderflower. It's well worth seeking out and fabulous as a gin and tonic with J.Gasco tonic water—another Italian import that's really balanced and delicious—but another London dry–style gin will work, too.

1 ounce Elena Gin

1 ounce Amaro Montenegro

½ ounce Combier Rose

½ ounce freshly squeezed lemon juice

½ ounce freshly squeezed
    grapefruit juice

¼ ounce simple syrup

3 dashes Regan's orange bitters

2 ounces Prosecco

Splash of tonic water, preferably
    J.Gasco brand

3 culinary-grade rose petals for garnish

1 green olive for garnish

Combine all the ingredients, up to the Prosecco, in a cocktail shaker filled with ice. Shake until the canister is frosty, then strain into a wineglass filled with ice. Top with the Prosecco and tonic water. Stir. Garnish with the rose petals and a green olive.

Snow in Summer

SERVES 1

Here, Nostrana bartender Russell Smith mingles bubbly Lambrusco with jammy liqueur in a refreshing play on the Kir Royale. Be sure to pick a dry rather than sweet Lambrusco to keep the drink from tasting syrupy.

¾ ounce Ketel One Vodka

¾ ounce Clear Creek Cassis

¾ ounce Lucano Amaro

½ ounce simple syrup

3 ounces dry red or rosé Lambrusco

Splash of soda water

5 frozen raspberries for garnish

2 large fresh mint sprigs for garnish

Powdered sugar for garnish

Combine all the ingredients, up to the Lambrusco, in a cocktail shaker filled with ice. Shake until the canister is frosty, then strain into a wineglass filled with ice. Top with the Lambrusco and soda water. Stir. Garnish with raspberries, mint sprigs, and a dusting of powdered sugar.

Zucchini Fritters

MAKES 8 FRITTERS

Everyone loves a fritter, but let's face it, some fritters are better than others. Unlike some heavier versions that trend toward pancakes, these are light and herbaceous, with just enough batter to hold the zucchini and herbs together. Serve them with a crisp white wine or some bubbles and raise a toast to the ever-versatile zucchini.

8 ounces medium zucchini (2 to 4 zucchini), grated (to yield 2 cups)

Sea salt

1 large egg

¼ cup loosely packed fresh mint leaves, 2 tablespoons fresh tarragon leaves, or a combination, chopped

¼ cup (30 g) all-purpose flour, plus more as needed

1 cup finely grated Parmigiano-Reggiano

Freshly ground black pepper

Extra-virgin olive oil for frying

Toss the grated zucchini with a generous pinch of salt in a colander. Allow to sit for 5 minutes, then squeeze the zucchini to remove the excess water until it is as dry as possible (you should end up with about 1 cup of zucchini).

Whisk the egg in a medium bowl. Add the zucchini, herbs, flour, cheese, 1 teaspoon of salt, and several grindings of pepper. Stir until well combined.

Line a baking sheet with paper towels to drain the fritters after frying and place near the stove.

Heat ½ inch of olive oil in a 12-inch skillet over medium heat until it reaches 350°F. Drop heaping tablespoon portions of the batter into the skillet, gently flatten with a spatula, and fry until golden brown, 2 minutes. Turn them over and repeat on the other side. Transfer to the prepared baking sheet and sprinkle lightly with salt while still hot. Repeat with the rest of the batter. Serve warm.

Fried Squash Blossoms
STUFFED WITH MOZZARELLA AND ANCHOVIES
SERVES 4 TO 6

When I see squash blossoms on a menu in any form, I have to order them. Part of the appeal is simply the crazy act of eating a big, palm-size flower. Then there's the visual beauty, so sunny yellow and delicately frilly. They're only available for a short time each summer and must be used the day they're picked; otherwise, the blossom closes up and wilts. Knowing how ephemeral they are just makes them all the more special.

Squash blossoms can be sliced and tossed into salads and pastas or strewn atop pizzas, but this preparation is my favorite by far. The flowers are stuffed with the very southern Italian combination of mozzarella and anchovies (or fresh basil for those who don't like anchovies), dipped in a white wine–based batter (inspired by one I found in *The Silver Spoon* cookbook), and deep-fried until light and crunchy. At Nostrana, whenever a server would go out in the dining room with a plate of these, we'd suddenly have a lot more orders for it. Since the blossoms are hard to find outside of growing your own, consider this recipe all the excuse you need to find room for a zucchini plant in the sunniest corner of your yard.

BATTER
1 cup (120 g) all-purpose flour
Sea salt
1 large egg, separated
⅓ cup white wine
2 tablespoons extra-virgin olive oil
⅔ cup warm water

BLOSSOMS
12 open zucchini flowers
4 ounces fresh mozzarella cheese, patted dry, cut into ½-inch-wide-sticks
3 salt-packed anchovies, rinsed, soaked, and filleted (see page xiv), or 12 fresh basil leaves
Extra-virgin olive oil for frying

continues

TO MAKE THE BATTER

Mix together the flour and a pinch of salt in a small bowl. Make a well in the center and add the egg yolk, white wine, olive oil, and warm water. Whisk these liquid ingredients together, then begin whisking in the flour until the ingredients are well blended. Cover with plastic wrap and let rest at room temperature for 1 hour.

Whisk the egg white with an electric mixer or by hand in a separate bowl until soft peaks form. Fold into the batter.

TO ASSEMBLE THE BLOSSOMS

Carefully pull the stamen from each zucchini flower and discard. Fill each flower with a stick of mozzarella and ½ anchovy fillet or basil leaf.

Heat 1 inch of oil in a deep sauté pan over medium-high heat until it reaches 360°F. Set a paper towel–lined baking sheet nearby.

Working in batches, carefully dip the flowers in the batter to coat well, then fry in the hot oil until golden brown, 3 to 6 minutes on each side. Remove with a slotted spoon and place on the paper towels. Sprinkle with salt while they're still hot. Serve immediately.

Grilled Shrimp
WITH HERBED RÉMOULADE
SERVES 4

(((((((((((((((((

Growing up in North Carolina, where we feasted on sweet Atlantic brown shrimp from the Carolina Coast from June through August, grilled shrimp with rémoulade always marked the official start of summer. Although piquant rémoulade sauce is a Cajun specialty with French roots, this herby version enriched with cooked egg yolks is much more Mediterranean in spirit. It's creamy but with a piccante profile similar to the herb sauces in the "Basics" chapter (which would be wonderful accompaniments to grilled shrimp, too).

RÉMOULADE

3 large eggs

1½ tablespoons red wine vinegar

1 teaspoon balsamic vinegar

1 teaspoon Dijon mustard

Sea salt

⅓ cup extra-virgin olive oil

⅓ cup finely chopped fresh flat-leaf parsley

⅓ cup minced fresh chives

2 tablespoons chopped fresh basil

1 tablespoon chopped fresh tarragon

2 tablespoons finely chopped cornichons

2 tablespoons salted capers (rinsed, soaked in cold water for 10 minutes, drained, and chopped)

GRILLED SHRIMP

1 pound shrimp (extra jumbo or 16/20)

2 tablespoons extra-virgin olive oil

Sea salt and freshly ground black pepper

TO MAKE THE RÉMOULADE

Fill a saucepan with just enough water to reach the bottom of a steamer basket or insert. Cover and bring to a boil over high heat. Add the eggs, cover, lower the heat to medium-high, and cook for 8 minutes (you want yolks that are cooked but slightly jammy). Transfer the eggs to a bowl of ice water to stop the cooking. Allow to cool in the ice water for 10 minutes.

Peel the eggs, cut in half, and scoop the yolks out into a bowl. (Save the whites to add to a salad or to snack on, or simply discard.) Use a fork to smash the egg yolks into a smooth consistency. Whisk in the red wine vinegar, balsamic vinegar, mustard, and a pinch of salt. Slowly whisk in the olive oil to create an emulsion. Gently fold in the remaining rémoulade ingredients. Taste and season with salt, if desired. Can be made up to 1 week ahead and refrigerated.

continues

TO GRILL THE SHRIMP

Peel the shrimp, leaving the tails on. Cut a slit along the curved back and remove the vein. Rinse and pat dry. In a bowl, toss the shrimp with the olive oil. Season with salt and pepper to taste. (Skewering the shrimp is optional but will make it easier to turn more of them at once; just make sure to soak any wooden skewers in water for at least 30 minutes before using and leave a little space between each shrimp to ensure they cook evenly.)

Prepare a grill for direct cooking over medium-high heat (400° to 450°F). Brush the cooking grates clean. Place the shrimp on the grates and cover with the lid. (Tip: If grilling unskewered shrimp, it helps to arrange them in an orderly way so you can keep track of which ones hit the grill first and remove them first to prevent overcooking.) Cook for 2 minutes, then turn them and cook on the other side for 2 to 3 minutes more, or until just cooked and no longer translucent in the center.

Transfer to a platter and serve with the rémoulade on the side.

Dandelion (or Radicchio) and Spring Red Onion Tortino

SERVES 4 TO 6

● ●

Tortino is similar to a frittata but thickened with flour and baked, giving it a slightly more cakey texture. Its forgettable appearance has also earned tortino the nickname "scarpaccia," which means "smashed old worn-out shoe," but it's really far more attractive than that. This version, adapted from Leslie Forbes's cookbook *A Taste of Tuscany*, is an ideal make-ahead appetizer cut into wedges or squares, or a lovely lunch or light dinner entrée that can accommodate whatever tender greens or leftover vegetables you have on hand.

¼ cup plus 3 tablespoons extra-virgin olive oil

2 large red spring onions, halved and sliced thinly

Sea salt

4 garlic cloves, sliced thinly

12 ounces dandelion or radicchio leaves, chopped coarsely

4 large eggs

2 tablespoons all-purpose flour

Freshly ground black pepper

Heat the 3 tablespoons of olive oil in a 10-inch, ovenproof, nonstick skillet (one that has a lid) over medium-low heat. Add the red spring onions and a pinch of salt. Sauté, tossing often, for 5 minutes. Add the garlic and continue to sauté until softened but still slightly crunchy, about 5 minutes more. Add the dandelion leaves and increase the heat to medium. Cover the pan and cook, tossing occasionally, until the leaves are tender and wilted, about 10 minutes. Remove from the heat, transfer the greens to a bowl, and let cool.

Preheat the oven to 500°F. Beat 1 egg in a large bowl until smooth. Sprinkle in the flour and mix to make a paste. Beat in the other 3 eggs, 1 teaspoon of salt, and ½ teaspoon of pepper until smooth. If the flour makes the mixture clumpy, pass the mixture through a fine sieve. Stir in the sautéed onions and greens.

Return the skillet to medium-low heat and add the remaining ¼ cup of olive oil. When hot, add the egg mixture and smooth the top with a spatula to help submerge any vegetables. Cook until set on the bottom and sides, about 6 minutes. Place the pan on the top rack of the oven. Bake for 3 minutes, or until the top is just set (it will not brown).

Remove from the oven and let cool for a few minutes before inverting onto a plate.

Cut into wedges and serve warm or at room temperature.

SALADS, SOUPS, AND SIDES

Zucchini Carpaccio
WITH TOMATO VINAIGRETTE
SERVES 4

When blessed with a prolific zucchini plant, don't fret that you're running out of ideas to use them up. Just pick them young and eat them raw in super-easy, super-fresh salads like this. Raw zucchini soaks up flavors like a champ, which is why this gorgeous and deeply flavored tomato vinaigrette is the perfect pairing. During tomato season, try blending in some roasted, peeled, and crushed tomatoes for added flavor. This recipe makes a bit more vinaigrette than you need, which is a good thing. It will keep in the fridge for about a week and is great as a dip for whole steamed artichokes or as a spread on sandwiches.

TOMATO VINAIGRETTE

¼ cup tomato paste

1 cup extra-virgin olive oil

1 garlic clove, minced finely or mashed in a mortar and pestle

¼ cup red wine vinegar (see Note)

¼ cup finely grated Parmigiano-Reggiano

¾ teaspoon salt

¼ teaspoon freshly ground black pepper

½ teaspoon dried Sicilian oregano

ZUCCHINI CARPACCIO

2 medium zucchini

12 ounces fresh mozzarella and/or burrata, torn into pieces (optional)

1 cup shaved Parmigiano-Reggiano

1 cup loosely packed fresh basil leaves, torn

Extra-virgin olive oil for drizzling

Sea salt and freshly ground black pepper

TO MAKE THE TOMATO VINAIGRETTE

Whisk together the tomato paste and ½ cup of the olive oil in a heavy-bottomed skillet or saucepan until well combined. Warm the mixture over low heat, stirring as needed to prevent sticking, for about 15 minutes, to infuse the oil with the tomato flavor. Keep the temperature low to prevent browning. Remove from the heat and let cool.

Whisk together the garlic, red wine vinegar, Parmesan, salt, pepper, and oregano in a medium bowl. Whisk this into the cooled tomato oil.

Gradually whisk in the remaining ½ cup of olive oil, starting with ¼ cup and adding more to taste, depending on the acidity level (you might not need to add the entire ½ cup).

Taste the vinaigrette and adjust the seasoning with more salt, olive oil, or vinegar, if desired. The texture will be quite thick. If you prefer a thinner consistency, whisk in a little water. Allow the vinaigrette to sit for at least an hour to allow the flavors to meld. (Makes about 1½ cups; will keep refrigerated for 1 week.)

TO MAKE THE ZUCCHINI CARPACCIO

Soak the zucchini in cold water for 20 minutes to hydrate and firm up. Slice the zucchini into ¼-inch-thick disks and arrange evenly on a large plate or platter. Sprinkle with salt and pepper. Add the mozzarella (if using). Spoon or drizzle about ¼ cup of the vinaigrette over the zucchini and cheese, adding more as necessary. The ingredients should be very well dressed but not submerged.

Scatter the shaved Parmesan and torn basil leaves over the platter. Drizzle with olive oil and season with salt and pepper. Serve with crusty bread to mop up all of the delicious vinaigrette.

• •

NOTE: *We like to use Katz brand Late Harvest Zinfandel Vinegar for this recipe. It's a sweet-and-sour vinegar that works great with the tomato flavor. If you can't find it, a pinch of sugar or spoonful of honey can help balance out more acidic, less fruity vinegars.*

Fresh Tomato, Peach, and Basil Salad
WITH STRACCIATELLA
SERVES 4

❛❛

Tomatoes and peaches work wonderfully well together—the sunny peaches pick up the sweetness of the tomatoes, while the richness of the tomatoes adds a bass note of savoriness that keeps things from tilting into dessert. Crisp sweet onions and radishes, earthy walnuts, and creamy cheese add exciting hits of complexity and texture. Stracciatella is the luscious mixture of cultured cream and fresh mozzarella strands—the same stuff that gets tucked into the middle of a ball of burrata. Here, it's dolloped onto the salad so it can intermingle with the ingredients, but you can also spread it on the bruschetta and top with the salad.

2 very large heirloom tomatoes	8 ounces stracciatella or burrata
2 ripe freestone peaches or nectarines	⅓ to ½ cup grassy extra-virgin olive oil
½ small sweet onion	1 small bunch radishes, excess greens
Flaky sea salt	and root ends trimmed, sliced
2 tablespoons red wine vinegar	½ cup fresh walnuts, toasted lightly
Freshly ground black pepper	(see Note)
8 to 12 large fresh basil leaves	4 slices Bruschetta (page 6), cut in half

Core the tomatoes and cut into ½-inch-thick slices. Cut the peaches in half and remove the pit. Slice into ¾-inch-thick wedges.

Peel the spring onion, cut in half vertically, then cut into ¼-inch-thick slices (this makes straighter, sticklike pieces rather than half-moons). Chill the slices in ice water for 10 minutes. Drain and squeeze dry in a clean kitchen towel.

Arrange the tomato and peach slices in an alternating pattern on a large serving platter. Distribute the sliced spring onion over the top.

Sprinkle the salad generously with salt (tomatoes need a good amount of salt) and let sit for 10 minutes to allow the salt to pull out some of the water, which will concentrate the flavors. Place a plate over the top to help you hold the ingredients in place as you tip the platter over the sink to drain off the watery juices.

Evenly sprinkle the red wine vinegar over the salad and season generously with pepper. Tear the basil and sprinkle evenly over the salad.

To serve, spoon dollops of the stracciatella on top of the salad or cut the burrata balls in half and distribute around the platter. Generously drizzle the salad with olive oil (start with the smaller amount and add more if needed. The salad should taste balanced—not too sharp and acidic and not too oily). Arrange the radishes and walnuts around. Serve with bruschetta.

• •

NOTE: *To toast walnuts, spread on a baking sheet and bake at 350°F for 8 to 10 minutes, until lightly golden.*

Insalata Nostrana

SERVES 8

This colorful take on Caesar salad was inspired by a dish I had a long time ago at Locanda Veneta Italian restaurant in Los Angeles. We've been making our version of it for so long now that it's become a signature dish. What makes it special is the use of deeply colored, slightly bitter radicchio in place of romaine. I find the most beautiful compact round heads of Rosso di Verona at the Portland farmers' market, but you can also use Treviso, which is torpedo-shaped like an endive, or Chioggia, which looks like Rosso di Verona but is rounder and more widely available at grocery stores. Although radicchio thrives in the winter, when cold temperatures increase its natural sugars, you can make this salad all summer long by soaking the radicchio in ice water for a couple of hours to tame the bitterness and make it refreshingly crisp. The other components—a creamy, anchovy-spiked dressing and crunchy, herb-flecked croutons—fill each bite with bold, exciting, contrasting flavors and textures. This might make more dressing than you need, but it keeps at least a week in the fridge and is great to have around for future salads, even grain salads.

DRESSING
3 tablespoons red wine vinegar

2 tablespoons white wine

2 tablespoons mayonnaise

4 oil-packed anchovies

2 large egg yolks

2 garlic cloves, pounded with a pinch of salt in a mortar and pestle until mashed

1 cup extra-virgin olive oil

Sea salt and freshly ground black pepper

CROUTONS
3 cups cubed focaccia (¾-inch cubes), flavored with sage, basil, or rosemary; or crusty artisan country bread

4 tablespoons (½ stick) unsalted butter

1 tablespoon chopped fresh sage

1 tablespoon chopped fresh rosemary

SALAD
2 to 3 heads radicchio (about 1 pound)

½ cup finely grated Parmigiano-Reggiano

TO MAKE THE DRESSING

Combine the red wine vinegar, white wine, mayonnaise, anchovies, egg yolks, and mashed garlic in a food processor. With the machine running, slowly add the oil and process briefly to emulsify. Season to taste with salt and pepper. (Makes about 1½ cups; will keep refrigerated for 1 week.)

TO MAKE THE CROUTONS

Preheat the oven to 375°F. Spread the bread cubes on a large baking sheet and bake, stirring and turning over with a spatula halfway through, until lightly browned, about 10 minutes. Remove from the oven.

Melt the butter in a large skillet over medium-low heat. Add the sage and rosemary and cook just until aromatic, about 1 minute. Remove from the heat, add the toasted bread cubes, toss well, and let cool. Once cooled, the croutons will keep in an airtight container for 2 days.

TO MAKE THE SALAD

Remove any damaged outer leaves from the radicchio, quarter it, cut out and discard the core, and tear into bite-size pieces. Soak in slightly iced water for 2 hours (even in winter it's a good idea to soak for at least an hour, as it crisps it up).

Drain the radicchio, dry it well, and put it into a large bowl. Toss with enough dressing to coat well. Add the croutons and toss. Divide the salad among plates, sprinkle with finely grated Parmesan, and serve.

Sicilian Potato Salad
(INSALATA PANTESCA)
WITH WILD OREGANO, CAPERS, AND OLIVES
SERVES 6

●●●●●● ●●● ● ●● ● ●●●●●●● ● ●●● ●● ● ●●●●●● ● ●● ● ●● ●●●●●

This is a very simple potato salad, but simple doesn't mean basic. A few easy tricks make all the difference. First, I boil the potatoes in their skins to keep them from getting waterlogged. The less water they absorb, the more flavor they can soak up later. As for the dressing, it's just oil and vinegar, but the key is adding the vinegar while the potatoes are still hot so they can pull in all that acidity while they cool. This is a recipe that benefits from the fruity or grassy flavor of olive oil, as it contrasts with the piquancy of the vinegar-soaked potatoes. It's wise to be generous when adding it. It's a really refreshing style of potato salad and much more suited to what you would want to eat in the summer than one cloaked in heavy mayonnaise.

6 medium (2 pounds total) Yukon Gold potatoes

Sea salt

½ medium white, red, or sweet onion, halved and sliced thinly

2 to 3 tablespoons red wine vinegar

4 large tomatoes, cut into 1-inch chunks, or 1 pint cherry tomatoes

½ cup pitted Gaeta or Cerignola olives, halved

1½ tablespoons salted capers, rinsed, soaked in cold water for 10 minutes, then drained

2 teaspoons dried Sicilian oregano, or 2 tablespoons fresh

½ to ¾ cup extra-virgin olive oil, plus more for serving

Place the potatoes in a large pot and cover with cold water by about 1 inch. Bring to a boil over high heat and salt generously. Lower the heat to medium and cook until tender but firm, about 25 minutes. Drain. Remove the skins while still warm but cool enough to handle, then cut the potato flesh into large chunks.

Place the warm potatoes and onion rings in a large bowl and sprinkle with the red wine vinegar. Let the potatoes absorb the liquid as they cool. Add the tomatoes, olives, capers, and oregano. Gently toss with ½ cup of olive oil until well combined, adding more, if necessary, to thoroughly coat. Season with salt to taste and add more vinegar if desired. This salad is best served at room temperature. Add another generous drizzle of oil before serving.

Seafood Salad
(INSALATA DI MARE)
SERVES 6

᙮᙮

Tiny pink bay shrimp and squid have so many things going for them. They're two of the most affordable and sustainable seafoods, and they're also fabulous at soaking up flavors, making them the ideal base for a fresh seafood salad tossed in a simple, herby vinaigrette. Poached plump mussels or sweet scallops are a great addition or substitution. In the many seafood restaurants that anchor the resorts along Italy's coasts, a salad like this would be a traditional appetizer followed by a first course of seafood pasta and a whole fish entrée. At home, I keep things much more simple, usually serving this alongside crusty grilled bread for a light lunch or dinner. Enjoy this with your toes in the sand as often as possible.

1 pound calamari	⅓ cup extra-virgin olive oil
Sea salt	Juice of ½ lemon (2 tablespoons), plus more as needed
1 teaspoon white wine vinegar	
1 pound bay (pink) shrimp	2 tablespoons chopped fresh flat-leaf parsley leaves
½ red onion, cut in half and sliced paper-thin	2 tablespoons chopped fresh basil
2 celery ribs, sliced thinly crosswise	2 tablespoons chopped fresh mint
2 garlic cloves	Freshly ground black pepper

If the calamari are whole, cut into thin rings, checking first to see that each one has no quill in it. Trim the tentacle sections by cutting off and discarding the flap of flesh below the tentacle "flower" and cutting the very long tentacle into a couple of pieces. Leave the small tentacle flowers whole and cut larger ones in half.

Bring a large saucepan of water to a boil. Season with salt and the white wine vinegar. Add the squid, partially cover with a lid, and bring back to a boil. Lower the heat to a simmer and cook for 20 minutes, or until tender (you may need to cook the squid up to 20 minutes more; test for doneness periodically). Drain and rinse with cold water to stop the cooking. Pat dry and set aside.

Rinse the bay shrimp in cold running water and pick through to remove any bits of shell. Pat dry and combine with the squid, sliced red onion, and celery in a medium bowl.

continues

Pound the garlic with a pinch of salt in a mortar and pestle to make a paste (alternatively, you can smash the garlic and salt on a cutting board with the side of a knife). Combine the garlic with the olive oil, lemon juice, and chopped herbs. Season with salt and pepper.

Pour the dressing over the seafood and mix thoroughly. Taste and add more salt, pepper, and lemon juice, if desired.

NOTE: The salad is best served immediately. If not planning to serve right away, make the dressing without the lemon juice, adding it to the dressed salad right before serving. That way, the acid in the lemon juice won't "cook" the fish. Keep the salad refrigerated until 30 minutes before serving. Taste again, add the lemon juice, and adjust the seasonings if necessary.

Rice and Bean Salad
(INSALATA DI RISO E FAGIOLI)
SERVES 4 TO 6 AS A MAIN DISH; 6 TO 8 AS A SIDE DISH

Here, chubby Carnaroli rice gets the pasta salad treatment. Instead of coaxing out its abundant starches through constant stirring, as we do with risotto, it's boiled like pasta, which gives it a satisfying chew, a loose texture, and allows for the rice's flavor to really shine through. Rustic croutons add even more texture, while the cavalcade of zingy additions, including olives, herbs, and anchovies, provides bright pops of flavor. You might be surprised to see the vinaigrette emboldened with a splash of dark rum. Similar to using vodka in tomato sauce, the alcohol in the rum heightens the flavors of the ingredients, and the natural sugars add a touch of balance. The salad itself is a blank slate—try adding sun-dried tomatoes or capers, canned tuna or bay shrimp, or roasted peppers or other roasted veggies preserved in oil. You can even use different varieties of rice, such as red or brown, or even farro. Think of this dish as a vehicle for piquant-tasting things that whet your appetite in the heat. Serve it alone as a main dish or alongside any grilled meat or seafood.

1 cup uncooked Carnaroli rice or farro

3 cups cooked cannellini beans, cooled and drained (see Perfect Beans, page 186)

2 small bunches scallions, white and light green parts only, sliced thinly

⅓ cup Taggiasca or Gaeta olives, or other flavorful black olives, pitted and halved

1½ cups halved cherry tomatoes

⅓ cup chopped fresh flat-leaf parsley leaves

1 tablespoon chopped fresh marjoram, or 2 tablespoons chopped fresh oregano

2 garlic cloves, minced

1 finely chopped oil-packed anchovy (optional)

¼ cup freshly squeezed lemon juice, plus more to taste

¼ cup dark rum

Sea salt and freshly ground black pepper

¾ cup extra-virgin olive oil

3 cups cubed Bruschetta (page 6; optional)

Line a baking sheet with several layers of paper towels.

Bring a large pot of salted water to a boil over high heat. Add the rice and cover the pot until the water returns to a boil. Remove the lid and continue to boil, stirring occasionally, for 10 to 15 minutes, or until the rice is al dente (you may need to cook longer if using farro).

Strain through a fine-mesh sieve and run under cold water until cool. Shake off the excess water and then spread the rice on the lined baking sheet. Allow to cool completely. The rice can be tossed with just enough olive oil to coat and keep it from sticking together, and refrigerated for up to 1 week.

Combine the cooked rice with the cooled beans, scallions, olives, cherry tomatoes, parsley, and marjoram in a large bowl.

Whisk together the garlic, anchovy (if using), lemon juice, and rum in a small bowl. Season with salt and pepper. Whisk in the olive oil until emulsified.

Drizzle the dressing over the salad and toss well to coat. Add the bread and toss again. Taste and add more salt, pepper, lemon juice, or olive oil, if desired (if using oil-cured olives, you may need more lemon juice).

Cannellini Bean and Grilled Tuna Salad
WITH GIARDINIERA
SERVES 4 TO 6

● ●

This hearty and colorful salad has been on the menu at Nostrana, in some form or another, since we opened. Customers love it so much we couldn't take it off the menu if we wanted to (and we don't). It's just one of those soul-satisfying dishes that checks all the boxes: it tastes good, looks good, and makes you feel good, too. We typically offer it as an antipasto at dinner, but it makes a lovely main course for lunch, especially when served with Bruschetta (page 6), and is ideal for picnics since it travels so well. At Nostrana, we use our oil-poached albacore conserva and white beans slowly cooked with garlic and sage until plump and flavorful, but canned beans and oil-packed tuna work great and require far less effort. This smoke-kissed version is our ode to summer, when fresh, Oregon-caught albacore tuna is in season and the outdoor grill is just begging to be put to use.

½ red onion, cut in half and sliced thinly

1½ pounds fresh albacore tuna

Extra-virgin olive oil

Sea salt and freshly ground black pepper

3½ cups cooked cannellini or corona beans (see Perfect Beans, page 186); or two 15-ounce cans cannellini beans, drained and rinsed

2 cups chopped giardiniera or other high-quality assorted (not sweet) pickled vegetables, such as carrots, radishes, bell peppers, and cauliflower

½ cup chopped fresh flat-leaf parsley leaves

1 handful alderwood chips (optional)

Red wine vinegar (optional)

Soak the red onion slices in cold water for 30 minutes, changing the water every 10 minutes and squeezing the slices occasionally, until the onion tastes mild and sweet. Drain well.

Prepare a grill for direct cooking over medium heat (350° to 400°F). Prepare a smoker box with alderwood chips, if desired, and place on the grill.

Cut the tuna into 6- to 7-ounce portions, 1 inch thick. Thoroughly pat the tuna dry, then brush with olive oil.

When the grill is ready, scrape the grates clean. Season the tuna with salt and black pepper and arrange the portions on the grates. Grill until seared, about 2 minutes. Turn them and sear the other

side, 1 to 2 minutes more. When cool enough to handle, break the tuna into large bite-size pieces and combine with the beans in a large bowl.

Drizzle the tuna and beans generously with olive oil until well coated. Add a few splashes of the pickling liquid from the giardiniera, or red wine vinegar, if preferred. Arrange the mixture on a platter and top with the sliced red onion, giardiniera, chopped parsley, and a few grinds of black pepper. Serve at room temperature.

Variation

In the spirit of carefree summer cooking, instead of grilling fresh tuna, you can use two small (5- or 6-ounce) cans of high-quality tuna packed in olive oil, drained (see page xx). Just remember: The higher the quality, the better the flavor, so don't be shy about splurging on the good stuff.

Chickpea and Olive Salad
WITH PAN-FRIED CALAMARI AND GREMOLATA
SERVES 4

From April through July, I keep my eyes open for the tiny pods of fresh chickpeas at farmers' markets and well-provisioned supermarkets in my area. Their appearance can be unpredictable, but it's always a cause for celebration. Lively green with a slightly grassy note, they're the ideal base for a summery salad with fresh herbs and tender calamari (or shrimp, if you prefer). But since fresh beans are so hard to come by, more often than not I use dried beans. They're just as delicious. Even canned will do just fine.

SALAD
4 ounces dried chickpeas, soaked overnight, or 2 cups cooked, or one 15-ounce can (see Note)

Sea salt

Zest and juice of 1 lemon

1 garlic clove, minced finely

3 tablespoons finely minced fresh flat-leaf parsley leaves

1 tablespoon chopped fresh thyme

Freshly ground black pepper

½ cup extra-virgin olive oil

1 cup cherry tomatoes, halved

¼ cup pitted oil-packed Taggiasca olives, halved

½ bunch scallions, white and light green parts only, sliced thinly

GREMOLATA
¼ cup chopped fresh flat-leaf parsley leaves

1 garlic clove, finely minced

Finely grated zest of 1 lemon

CALAMARI
½ cup (60 g) all-purpose flour

Sea salt and freshly ground black pepper

8 ounces calamari, cut into rings (or medium shrimp, peeled and deveined)

Vegetable oil for frying

TO MAKE THE SALAD
Drain the dried chickpeas and place in a medium saucepan. Add enough water to cover by 2 to 3 inches. Bring to a boil over medium-high heat, season generously with salt, and lower the heat to low. Simmer until tender, 1 to 2 hours depending on the age of the chickpeas.

Meanwhile, combine the lemon zest and juice, garlic, parsley, and thyme in a medium bowl. Season with salt and pepper. Slowly whisk in the oil. Taste and add more salt and pepper, if desired.

When the chickpeas are tender, drain and salt lightly. Add to the oil mixture while still hot. Add the tomatoes, olives, and scallions. Toss well, taste, and adjust the seasoning, if desired.

TO MAKE THE GREMOLATA
Combine all the gremolata ingredients in a small bowl.

TO MAKE THE CALAMARI
Place the flour in a shallow bowl and toss with enough salt and pepper to season it well. Dredge the calamari in the seasoned flour. Transfer to a colander and toss over the sink to shake off the excess.

Heat ¼ inch of vegetable oil in a 10-inch skillet over medium-high heat until hot but not smoking (350° to 375°F). Add the calamari and sauté, stirring, until crisp and golden, 1 to 2 minutes (2 to 4 minutes if using shrimp). Transfer with a slotted spoon to a paper towel–lined plate to drain.

To serve, shower the calamari with the gremolata and serve alongside or on top of the chickpea salad.

* *

NOTE: To use fresh, shelled chickpeas, bring a large pot of water to a boil over high heat and salt generously. Add the fresh beans and cook until tender, about 3 minutes. Use a skimmer or slotted spoon to transfer to a colander and rinse under cold water until just warm. If using precooked or canned chickpeas, heat them with their liquid in a small saucepan until warm, then drain.

Grilled Vegetable Platter
WITH STUFFED PEPPERS
SERVES 6 TO 8

●●●

A platter piled with an assortment of grilled vegetables is a great side dish for a backyard dinner party, especially when served with an assortment of piquant, herby sauces (see the "Basics" chapter). It can be made a few hours in advance and left at room temperature, and it gives your guests a chance to pick and choose their favorites. Just add some grilled sausages or other grilled protein for a full meal. I'll readily admit, however, that I am just as happy eating these silky and slightly smoky vegetables on their own with a few slices of bruschetta hot off the grill and some cool and creamy balls of fresh mozzarella or burrata for a luscious contrast. The leftover vegetables are wonderful in sandwiches and pasta salads, too. A big thank-you to my good friend Bruce Aidells for sharing his marinade recipe with me.

MARINADE
1 cup extra-virgin olive oil
½ cup freshly squeezed lemon juice
5 garlic cloves, chopped finely
3 tablespoons chopped fresh basil
3 tablespoons chopped fresh oregano
Sea salt and coarsely ground black
   pepper

VEGETABLES
2 medium zucchini
4 small Japanese eggplants
2 yellow bell peppers
2 red bell peppers
2 small heads radicchio, preferably
   Treviso

2 portobello mushrooms, stems
   removed
Extra-virgin olive oil
1 bunch green onions
8 to 10 thin slices pancetta
1 cup cherry tomatoes, quartered
1 large shallot, chopped finely
1 tablespoon finely chopped fresh
   flat-leaf parsley
1 large garlic clove, thinly sliced
3 anchovy fillets, torn into small pieces

ASSEMBLY
6 to 8 slices Bruschetta (page 6)
Eggplant Puree (page 173; optional)
Fresh basil, gently torn, for garnish

TO MAKE THE MARINADE
Combine all the marinade ingredients in a large bowl (large enough to hold the zucchini and eggplant), season with salt and black pepper to taste, and whisk until emulsified.

TO PREPARE THE VEGETABLES

Soak the zucchini in cold water for 20 minutes to hydrate and firm up. Rinse, pat dry, and slice lengthwise into ½-inch-thick planks.

Trim the tops off the Japanese eggplants and slice each eggplant in half lengthwise.

Cut the red and yellow bell peppers into quarters lengthwise and remove the stem and seeds.

Cut the radicchio in half lengthwise and make several slits in the core.

Add the zucchini, eggplant, bell peppers, and mushrooms to the bowl of marinade and toss to coat. Allow to marinate for 5 to 10 minutes. Remove with a slotted spoon and place on a rimmed baking sheet; reserve the marinade. Place the radicchio on the baking sheet and brush with olive oil.

While the vegetables marinate, trim the root end off the green onions, slice about an inch off the green tops, and peel away the outer layer. Wrap a slice of pancetta up the length of each green onion, covering most of it.

Prepare a grill for direct cooking over medium heat (350° to 400°F). Scrub the cooking grates clean. Arrange the peppers on the grill. Cook until grill marks appear, about 5 minutes. Turn them over and repeat on the other side. Transfer to the baking sheet.

Arrange the pancetta-wrapped onions on the grill, perpendicular to the slats in the grates, and cook until the pancetta is nicely browned, about 5 minutes. Transfer to a large serving platter (leave plenty of room for the other vegetables and bruschetta).

Grill the remaining marinated vegetables until grill marks appear on both sides (4 to 6 minutes for zucchini and eggplant, 8 to 10 minutes for mushrooms). Transfer to the platter as they finish cooking.

Rearrange the coals (or turn off a burner) for indirect cooking. Distribute the quartered cherry tomatoes among the hollows of the grilled bell peppers. Sprinkle with chopped shallot, parsley, thinly sliced garlic, and anchovies. Drizzle with extra-virgin olive oil. Place the peppers on the cool side of the grill, cover, and cook until the tomatoes and oil sizzle, about 20 minutes. Transfer to the platter and garnish with torn basil.

When ready to serve, arrange the bruschetta around the platter or set on a separate serving plate.

To serve, clear a space on the platter for a mound of the eggplant puree (if using). Drizzle the remaining marinade over the vegetables and serve.

Rob's Summery Braised Cabbage

SERVES 4 TO 6

Cabbage doesn't exactly scream summertime, but trust me, this lovely side dish zested up with lemon and fresh mint offers all the bright and lively flavors we crave this time of year. The recipe comes from Rob Roy (yes, his real name), Nostrana's talented and longtime macellaio (butcher), who broke down all of our meats for more than a decade. You can use any variety of cabbage, but I prefer the frilly, ruffly savoy variety because it's milder and sweeter than regular green or red cabbage, and it gets even more nutty and sweet with cooking. Farmers' markets will likely have other heirloom varieties that are worth a try, such as arrowhead cabbage, with its crazy pointed top. Cabbage sounds unsexy, but once you get past the fuddy-duddy name, it's easy to fall for this produce aisle wallflower. It's inexpensive, keeps for a long time, is super good for you, and tastes wonderful raw in crunchy slaws and silky, sweet, and nutty when cooked as it is here. As delicious as it is on its own, it makes a great lunch when piled atop toasted artisan bread with a poached egg and a shower of grated Parmesan.

Sea salt

1 large head savoy cabbage

¼ cup extra-virgin olive oil, plus more for serving

4 garlic cloves, minced finely

5 tablespoons freshly squeezed lemon juice

2 tablespoons finely chopped fresh mint

2 tablespoons finely chopped fresh flat-leaf parsley leaves

1 tablespoon lemon zest

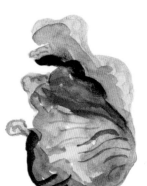
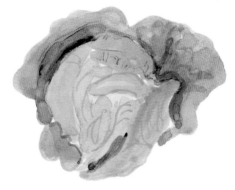

Bring a large stockpot of water to a boil over high heat. Season with a generous amount of salt (it should taste pleasantly like seawater).

Cut the cabbage in half and cut out the hard core near the base. Slice the cabbage crosswise into ½-inch-wide strips. Blanch the cabbage in the boiling water for 1 minute, drain or remove with a slotted spoon, then spread out on a baking sheet.

Heat the olive oil in a large, high-sided sauté pan over medium heat. Add the garlic and cook, stirring, until softened but not brown, 1 to 2 minutes. Add the lemon juice and cabbage, increase the heat to medium-high, and sauté for about 5 minutes, stirring often, until cabbage is wilted. Add the mint, parsley, lemon zest, and a few pinches of salt. Taste and add more salt or lemon juice, as needed. Serve immediately, drizzled with more olive oil.

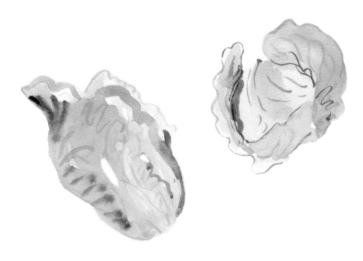

Artichokes alla Romana

SERVES 4

• •

A long, slow simmer in a generous bath of white wine and olive oil transforms prickly artichokes into a luscious side dish that practically melts in your mouth. When preparing these edible thistles, it's important to remove anything dark green. Although you might be alarmed by the volume of trimmings destined for the compost bin, those leaves will be too fibrous to eat anyway, and you'll be rewarded with a whole, tender, entirely edible artichoke imbued with the flavors of mint, parsley, and olive oil. Just be sure not to cut off the stem, which, when peeled, is as delicious as the prized artichoke heart itself.

1½ lemons

4 large artichokes

⅓ cup minced fresh mint

⅓ cup minced fresh flat-leaf parsley

2 garlic cloves, minced

½ cup extra-virgin olive oil

Sea salt

½ cup white wine with good acidity, or more as needed

Squeeze the juice from the ½ lemon into a large bowl of cold water, then drop in the lemon, too. Cut the remaining lemon into wedges and reserve for serving. Cut off the top third of each artichoke. Working with one artichoke at a time, snap off all the tough leaves until you reach the tender inner leaves that are the palest green and yellow. You have to be brutal: There should be nothing left that's darker than the palest green leaf. With a paring knife or vegetable peeler, peel away the tough, dark green outer layer of the stem and base until all that's left is pale green. Open up the center of the leaves and use a spoon (a grapefruit spoon works great for this) to scrape and dig out the purplish thistlelike choke. Place the cleaned artichokes in the lemon water as you go to prevent discoloration.

Combine the herbs, garlic, ¼ cup of the olive oil, and ¼ teaspoon of salt in a small bowl. Distribute a generous spoonful of the herb mixture between the leaves of each artichoke and the heart. Reserve the remaining herb mixture.

Arrange the artichokes, stem up, in a heavy nonreactive pot just large enough to hold them snugly. Sprinkle the remaining herb mixture over them and drizzle with the remaining ¼ cup of olive oil. Pour in the wine to a depth of ½ inch.

Cover the pot and place over medium heat. When the liquid reaches a boil, lower the heat to low. Put a clean, folded towel or piece of parchment paper between the lid and pot, cover again, and place a weight on the lid (these extra steps are to ensure a tight seal). Cook over low heat until artichokes are very tender and a knife slides in and out easily, about 40 minutes.

When the artichokes are tender, uncover the pot and let the juices boil away until only the oil remains, allowing the artichokes to cook for a few minutes in just the oil. Serve warm or at room temperature with lemon wedges.

Peperonata

MAKES 3½ CUPS

Sicilian agrodolce isn't just a sour-sweet condiment or sauce; it's also a tradition—a hallmark of the cuisine. The practice of slapping savory foods awake with a splash of vinegar, then taming the shrill tartness with a pinch of sugar, maybe even some raisins or honey, is what makes the eggplant in caponata and the roasted peppers in this peperonata so downright irresistible. You'll want to spoon this over everything—toasty bruschetta, polenta, grilled summer vegetables, cold roasted meat, rotisserie chicken, fried eggs. It even makes a great pizza topping.

2 large red bell peppers

2 large yellow bell peppers

3 tablespoons extra-virgin olive oil

1 large onion, sliced thinly

2 garlic cloves, peeled and sliced thinly

1 cup tomato puree or peeled and chopped fresh tomato

1 to 2 tablespoons red wine vinegar

2 teaspoons mild-tasting honey, or as needed

Sea salt and freshly ground black pepper

Prepare a grill for direct cooking over medium-high heat (400° to 450°F). Arrange the bell peppers on the cooking grate and grill until charred, about 10 minutes. Turn them and continue to grill until charred on all sides, about 10 more minutes total. Place the peppers in a clean paper bag and fold the top to seal, or place in a bowl and cover with plastic wrap. Let the peppers cool for about 20 minutes as the trapped steam loosens the skins.

Alternatively, preheat the oven to 450°F. Arrange the bell peppers on a baking sheet and roast until the surfaces are charred and wrinkled, about 10 minutes. Turn them over and repeat on the other side. Remove from the heat and cover the baking sheet tightly with foil to steam.

When the bell peppers are cool enough to handle, use your fingers to peel off the charred skins. Remove the stems, cut the peppers in half, and remove the seeds. (Resist the urge to rinse them, as it removes a lot of flavor.) Cut the peeled peppers into 1-inch-wide strips.

Heat the olive oil in a large sauté pan over medium-low heat. Add the onion and sauté until limp, 8 to 10 minutes. Add the garlic and sauté for 1 minute more. Add the grilled peppers and sauté, stirring, for 3 minutes. Add the tomato puree, lower the heat to low, and cook until the mixture thickens, about 30 minutes. Taste and add the vinegar and honey, enough to give it a pleasant sweet-and-sour taste. Season with salt and black pepper. Serve at room temperature.

Eggplant Caponata

SERVES 8 TO 10

ⲥ ⲥ

Looking at this recipe, you might wonder why the eggplant is roasted on its own, and why the celery is poached and then sautéed separately from everything else. You might be tempted to cut down on the dirty dishes and cook everything in the same pot. It all goes there in the end, right? But if you did, you'd be missing out on what makes this particular caponata so vibrant and interesting. It is not a pot of stewed vegetables. Instead, every component both stands out and melds together, like a jazz performance where everyone gets a solo. There's the poached celery and roasted eggplant, the sweet onions and raisins and bright tomatoes, the salty olives and briny capers and nutty pignoli. All of these different textures and contrasts and flavors add up to a very complex dish. I've made other caponata recipes, but I always come back to this one that I first learned to make at Portland's Genoa restaurant. Be sure to make it several hours ahead to allow the flavors to meld before serving.

2 large eggplants (2 pounds total), cut into 1-inch cubes

¾ cup plus 1 tablespoon extra-virgin olive oil

Sea salt and freshly ground black pepper

3 large tomatoes

5 celery ribs, cut into thin, 2-inch-long matchsticks

3 medium red onions, halved and sliced thinly

8 ounces (1 cup) Gaeta olives, drained, pitted, and sliced in half

¼ cup salted capers, rinsed, soaked in water for 10 minutes, and drained

2 tablespoons golden raisins

2 tablespoons pine nuts

¼ cup red wine vinegar

1 tablespoon honey

Preheat the oven to 450°F. Line two baking sheets with parchment paper.

Toss the eggplant with ½ cup of the olive oil in a large bowl until well coated. Arrange in a single layer, not touching, on the prepared baking sheets. Roast until cooked through, lightly browned, and tender but not mushy, about 30 minutes, stirring halfway through. Season with salt and pepper to taste.

Meanwhile, bring a medium saucepan of water to a boil over high heat. Place a bowl of ice water nearby. Score an X in the bottom of the tomatoes and add to the boiling water. Blanch until the skins begin to loosen, 30 seconds to a minute. Remove with a slotted spoon and plunge into the ice water to stop the cooking. Transfer to a cutting board, slice in half, and peel off the skins. Gently remove the juice and seeds with your fingers. Coarsely chop the tomatoes by hand.

Return the water to a boil, add a pinch of salt, and add the celery. Cook until just tender, about 5 minutes. Remove with a slotted spoon and plunge into the ice water to stop the cooking. Drain.

Heat ¼ cup of the olive oil in a large sauté pan over medium-high heat. Add the red onions and sauté until softened and just beginning to color, about 10 minutes. Add the chopped tomato along with the olives, capers, raisins, and pine nuts. Cover, lower the heat to a simmer, and cook for 15 minutes.

Heat the remaining tablespoon of olive oil in a medium sauté pan over medium heat. Add the celery and sauté for a few minutes, or until tender-crisp. Add the red wine vinegar and honey; simmer until no liquid remains, about 10 minutes.

Stir the celery and roasted eggplant into the tomato mixture and season with salt and pepper. Let stand at room temperature for several hours to allow the flavors to meld. (Can be refrigerated for up to 5 days. Allow to come to room temperature before serving.)

Pappa al Pomodoro, Winemaker Style

SERVES 6

Italians really know how to celebrate perfect fresh tomatoes. They also know how to ingeniously use every scrap of food, and this classic summer dish is one more delicious example of both. It uses torn pieces of stale artisan bread that become silky and almost custardy as they soak in the tomatoey broth. Pappa means "baby food" in Italian, a reference to the desired texture of the dish, which is puddinglike—it should sit up in the spoon. Honestly, I like it a little more brothy; if you do, too, just add more tomatoes or broth. Some people serve it hot, but room temperature will bring out all the flavor and keep the texture lush, making it a great make-ahead dish. I'll confess, however, that I do eat cold leftovers directly from the fridge.

Every year, I travel to my friend's olive orchard outside Cortona in Tuscany to help pick the olives, and I always end up making this soup. One year, I was cooking for 18 pickers, and even though I scaled it up like crazy, when I walked over to the pot to ladle some out into my own bowl, it was all gone. It's just that good.

This version is seasoned with a hint of fresh ginger, which is a twist I first tasted when winemaker Michael Falchini made it for a big dinner at his family winery in San Gimignano. I've made it this way ever since.

⅓ cup extra-virgin olive oil

2 cups thinly sliced leek, white and light green parts, or sliced red spring onions

2 garlic cloves, sliced

1 tablespoon finely grated fresh ginger, or more to taste

3 pounds fresh ripe tomatoes, peeled, seeded, and chopped (see "How to Peel Tomatoes," page 181)

Leaves from 1 small bunch fresh basil (about 1 loosely packed cup)

Sea salt and freshly ground black pepper

3 to 4 cups homemade or low-sodium canned chicken broth, or water, or more to taste

½ loaf stale white, whole wheat, or country bread (about 8 ounces), crusts removed, torn into 1- to 1½-inch pieces (about 5 lightly packed cups)

Grassy, full-flavored extra-virgin olive oil for drizzling

Heat the olive oil in a large saucepan over medium heat. Add the leek and gently sauté until tender, about 10 minutes (don't let it brown). Add the garlic and ginger and sauté for a couple minutes more.

Add the tomatoes and half of the basil leaves, and season with salt and several twists of pepper. Cook until the tomatoes soften, about 10 minutes. Add the broth, bring to a boil, and cook for another minute or two.

Remove the tomatoes from the heat, fold in the bread, cover, and let rest for 1 hour. The bread should have absorbed all the juices and be extremely moist and tender; if there are still dry bits, moisten with a touch more water. In Italy, some versions of this soup are so thick you can almost stand a spoon in them. Feel free to thin out the soup to your preference. Taste and adjust the seasoning, if desired.

Spoon into wide bowls, drizzle with a good dose of olive oil, tear the remaining basil leaves into pieces and distribute them over the top.

Italian Roasted Potatoes

SERVES 4 TO 6

Boiling the potatoes before roasting ensures they cook up fluffy and tender inside, crispy outside, and not at all dried out and leathery. A generous shower of salt and fresh herbs is all they need to become the little black dress of side dishes. Created by Nostrana's event chef, Sara Woods, these potatoes go with nearly any Italian or Mediterranean-inspired main dish, from deeply savory porchetta and Bistecca alla Fiorentina (page 54) to a light and simple grilled salmon. They make a lovely brunch accompaniment, too.

2½ pounds Yukon Gold potatoes, cut into 1½-inch chunks or wedges

Sea salt

⅓ cup extra-virgin olive oil

4 garlic cloves, minced

5 fresh sage leaves, minced

4 parsley sprigs, minced

Leaves from 2 rosemary sprigs, minced

Freshly ground black pepper

Preheat the oven to 425°F. Place the potatoes in a large pot and cover with cold water by about 1 inch. Bring to a boil over high heat and salt generously. Lower the heat to medium and cook until just tender, 6 to 7 minutes. Drain in a colander and let steam until dry, about 5 minutes. Transfer the potatoes to a large bowl and toss with the olive oil, garlic, sage, parsley, and rosemary. Season with salt and pepper. Spread in a single layer on a baking sheet. Roast for 30 minutes, or until golden brown and crispy on the bottom.

Pappa di Zucchini

SERVES 4

● ●

This soft, luscious puree is like a warm summer evening in a bowl, and it's lovely topped with briny ricotta salata and fresh basil. As with Pappa al Pomodoro (page 52), the texture should be thick enough to stand up like a soft little mound in your spoon. But this version doesn't need bread to thicken it. The flavors are best enjoyed when the soup is served just warm or at room temperature, not piping hot, which makes the soup especially suited to summer.

¾ cup extra-virgin olive oil, plus more for drizzling

3 pounds zucchini, ends trimmed, sliced into ½-inch-thick rounds

Sea salt and freshly ground pepper

2 large yellow onions, chopped finely

3 tablespoons chopped fresh oregano or marjoram

Pinch of red pepper flakes

About 1 cup water

Ricotta salata for garnish

Fresh basil for garnish

Heat 3 tablespoons of the oil in a deep 12-inch sauté pan over medium heat. Add enough zucchini in a single layer to cover the bottom of the pan without crowding, and season with salt and pepper. Sauté, turning occasionally, until lightly colored and tender enough to easily crush against the side of the pan, 10 to 15 minutes. Transfer the cooked zucchini to a large saucepan or Dutch oven. Repeat with the remaining zucchini, adding more oil when necessary.

When the zucchini is cooked, return the sauté pan to medium-low heat (if necessary, clean the pan) and add 3 more tablespoons of the olive oil. Add the onion, oregano, and red pepper flakes, and season with salt and black pepper. Sauté the onion gently, taking care not to let it brown (add a little water if starting to brown), until utterly soft and sweet, about 20 minutes. Add the cooked onion to the zucchini in the stockpot. Pour in any remaining olive oil.

At this point, the zucchini mixture will be very soft and juicy. Use an immersion blender to roughly puree the soup in the pot, adding about ½ cup to 1 cup of water so that it blends and collapses into a very thick soup. (Alternatively, puree the soup in batches, using a blender.) Add a little more water, if needed. The soup should be thick enough to stand up in the spoon, not liquidy or watery.

Return the pureed soup to the stove and reheat gently over medium heat, stirring frequently, until it simmers. Taste and adjust the seasoning, if necessary.

Serve the soup gently warmed rather than piping hot, with a generous drizzle of olive oil, a shaving of ricotta salata, and torn basil.

Minestrone alla Milanese

SERVES 6 TO 8

Few want to eat a hot bowl of soup on a sweltering summer's day, but cooled soup is a different story. In Milan, they'll cook pots of minestrone in the breezy morning hours, using all the vegetables from the garden, then perch the pots on the windowsill until they cool down for lunch. One summer, I made this soup with an array of Technicolor vegetables from my CSA box—purple carrots, yellow pole beans, variegated cabbage. The result was a psychedelic-looking bowl that was as amazing to look at as it was to eat. If you want a soup that similarly surprises and delights, go to the farmers' market and seek out the most colorful vegetables you can find, and try using water instead of broth so you can really taste the essence of each one. You can certainly used canned beans in this, but I think freshly cooked are even better. Just be sure to plan a couple days ahead.

¼ cup extra-virgin olive oil

1 small onion, diced (about ½ cup)

1 medium carrot, peeled and diced (about ½ cup)

1 large celery rib, diced (about ½ cup)

Sea salt

2 garlic cloves, minced

½ small cabbage (about 8 ounces), cored, shredded, and chopped

4 cups chicken or vegetable broth

1 cup tomato puree or crushed tomatoes

2 medium zucchini, cut into ¼-inch cubes

1 large potato, peeled and cut into ¼-inch cubes

¼ cup chopped fresh flat-leaf parsley leaves

8 ounces green beans, ends trimmed, cut into ½-inch lengths

4 cups Perfect Beans (page 186), ideally borlotti or cannellini beans, and the cooking liquid

½ cup uncooked Carnaroli or Arborio rice

4 cups water, or more as needed

4 to 6 tablespoons Basil Pesto (page 175) for serving

Fresh basil for garnish

Extra-virgin olive oil for drizzling

continues

Heat the olive oil in a large pot or Dutch oven over medium heat. Add the onion, carrot, and celery and season with salt. Sauté until softened, about 15 minutes. Add the garlic, lower the heat to medium-low, and sauté until fragrant, about 2 minutes. Add the cabbage and sauté until wilted, about 10 minutes.

Add the chicken broth, tomato puree, zucchini, potato, parsley, and green beans. Season with salt. Bring to a boil over medium-high heat, lower the heat to medium-low, and simmer, uncovered, for 20 to 30 minutes.

Add the cooked beans and their liquid, rice, and 4 cups of water. Increase the heat and simmer until the rice is just tender, 15 to 18 minutes. Add more water if desired. Remove from the heat and let cool to room temperature.

To serve, divide the soup among bowls, swirl a tablespoon of pesto into each, sprinkle with torn basil, and drizzle with olive oil.

Sage and Black Bean Soup
WITH BRUSCHETTA
SERVES 6

When Nostrana first opened, I got amazing black beans from Ayers Creek Farm that immediately brought to mind Zuppa Bastarda, a black bean soup from the 1996 cookbook *Zuppa* by Anne Bianchi. The questionable nickname for black beans (bastarda) was inspired by the fascists in Italy, who wore black shirts and were called bastards. It's an ironic name for a soup that gives you the freedom to choose three different ways to serve it. Four, actually, if you just eat it plain. So, I've given the soup my own twists and a new name, too. Carol and Anthony Boutard, friends and former owners of Ayers Creek Farm, loved this earthy soup so much they put it in their popular newsletter. Garnished with fresh tomatoes, basil, and rustic garlicky toasts, there's definitely a lot to love.

½ cup extra-virgin olive oil, plus more
for serving

8 shallots, minced

3 garlic cloves, minced

4 cups cooked black beans (see Perfect
Beans, page 186), with their broth

12 fresh sage leaves, chopped finely

Sea salt and freshly ground black pepper

Bruschetta con Salsa di Pomodoro
(page 6)

Basil Pesto (page 175; optional)

Heat the oil in a large stockpot over medium-high heat. Add the shallots and sauté until softened and golden, about 5 minutes. Add the garlic and sauté until fragrant, about 2 minutes.

Drain the beans and reserve their liquid. Add the beans to the stockpot, plus enough bean liquid (about 4 cups) to achieve the consistency you like for your soup. Reserve any remaining bean liquid, as you may want to thin out the soup later. Bring to a simmer and cook for 15 minutes.

continues

Add the chopped sage. Season with salt and pepper. Transfer one-third of the soup to a blender and puree (keep the lid ajar to let steam escape) or use an immersion blender. Mix the pureed beans back into the soup. Adjust the consistency with more bean broth, vegetable or chicken broth, or water, if you like, especially if you plan to serve it on top of the toasts.

To serve, you have three options:

1. Place a garlic toast in each soup bowl. Spoon the bean soup over the toast and garnish generously with the salsa. Drizzle with olive oil.

2. Divide the soup among bowls. Top the toasts with the salsa and set on or against the rim of the bowl. Drizzle with olive oil.

3. Serve as in option #1 or #2 and garnish with pesto.

Ligurian Seafood Stew
(CACCIUCCO)
SERVES 6

Cioppino is a seafood stew most Americans have at least heard of if not enjoyed many times over. But when I mention "cacciucco" I tend to get blank stares, which is funny, considering they're almost the same thing. Cacciucco is a classic dish from Liguria, the Tuscan port city on the coast of the Italian Riviera, and was created by Ligurian fishermen to use up the odds and ends of the day's catch. In fact, it's commonly said that the dish must contain five different kinds of fish—one for each "c" in the name. Generations later and 6,000 miles away, Ligurian immigrants working as fishermen in San Francisco did the same thing but called their version cioppino. Why the new name? Perhaps it was the addition of Dungeness crab, a California coast staple. Or the swap of white wine instead of red (Tuscans almost exclusively cook with red wine). Maybe it was the bread—Tuscan bread is unsalted and goes stale in a jiffy, so it gets tucked at the bottom of the bowl for serving, whereas cioppino is always served with grilled sourdough bread on the side. Whatever you call it, feel free to get in the spirit of tradition and use whatever seafood looks good at the market that day.

SOUP BASE
⅓ cup extra-virgin olive oil

1 small onion, diced

1 carrot, peeled and diced

1 celery rib, diced

3 garlic cloves, minced

2 bay leaves

2 fresh flat-leaf parsley sprigs

¼ to ½ teaspoon red pepper flakes, or 2 small dried chiles, to taste

1 cup red wine, such as Chianti

2 cups tomato puree or passato

1 quart fish broth

MARINATED FISH
1½ pounds mixed skinless, boneless white fish, such as petrale sole, halibut, and black cod

8 ounces dry-packed scallops, side muscle removed

¼ cup fresh flat-leaf parsley leaves, chopped

3 tablespoons extra-virgin olive oil

Sea salt and freshly ground black pepper

FOR SERVING
3 slices Bruschetta (page 6), cut in half

18 clams, cleaned

18 mussels, cleaned

1 lemon, cut into wedges

Chopped fresh flat-leaf parsley for garnish

Extra-virgin olive oil for drizzling

continues

TO MAKE THE SOUP BASE

Heat the olive oil in a large Dutch oven (it should be big enough to eventually contain the 2 pounds of fish and seafood) over medium heat. Add the onion, carrot, and celery. Sauté until softened and golden, about 12 minutes. Add the garlic and sauté for 1 minute more. Add the bay leaves, parsley, and red pepper flakes. Sauté for 1 minute. Add the red wine, stirring to scrape up any browned bits, and cook for 5 minutes. Add the tomato puree and cook for 10 minutes more. Add the fish broth, bring to a boil, lower the heat to a simmer, and cook for 10 minutes.

TO MARINATE THE FISH

While the soup base is simmering, cut the fish into 2-inch pieces. Gently toss with the scallops, parsley, and olive oil in a bowl. Season with salt and black pepper. Allow to marinate for 30 minutes.

TO SERVE

Remove the parsley stems and bay leaves. Add the thicker pieces of fish (such as the halibut and black cod) to the simmering soup base. Cook for a few minutes, or until halfway done. Add the petrale sole and scallops and cook for 2 minutes more. Turn off the heat.

Divide the bruschetta among six warmed soup bowls. Using a slotted spoon or spider, divide the fish among the bowls. Return the broth to a simmer and add the clams and mussels. Remove them with a slotted spoon as they open, 2 to 4 minutes, and divide them among the bowls.

Ladle the broth into the bowls. Squeeze the lemon wedges over the soup and sprinkle with parsley. Drizzle generously with olive oil and serve.

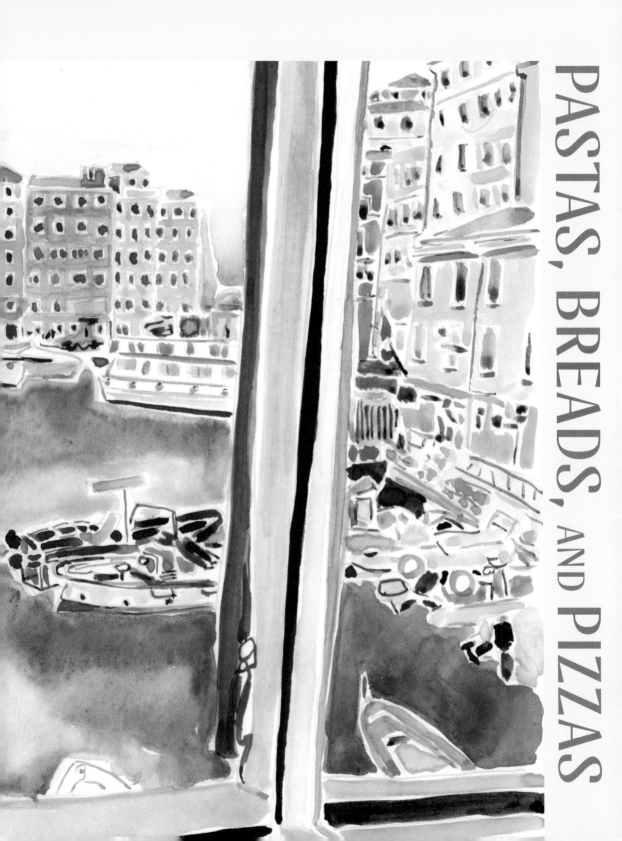

PASTAS, BREADS, AND PIZZAS

Pasta alla Checca

SERVES 4 TO 6

Wait until the height of summer, when tomatoes are at their juicy best, to put this pasta on regular rotation. A traditional Roman dish, it's simply composed of raw tomatoes marinated with basil, garlic, and olive oil, which means top-notch tomatoes are crucial to its success. Add a tangle of hot spaghetti, toss well, and dinner's on the table. I add olives and red pepper flakes for a little extra punch, and I often let the pasta cool before mixing to create a room-temperature dish ideal for sweltering summer nights.

2 pounds very ripe and juicy tomatoes, chopped coarsely, or halved cherry tomatoes

Sea salt

½ cup extra-virgin olive oil

1 cup torn fresh basil leaves

4 garlic cloves, sliced very thinly

¼ to ½ teaspoon red pepper flakes or Calabrian chiles in oil, or 1 fresh chile, such as jalapeño or serrano, seeded and chopped finely

⅓ cup pitted whole Taggiasca or Gaeta olives, quartered (see Note)

1 pound uncooked spaghetti

Flaky sea salt for garnish

Toss the tomatoes with about ½ teaspoon of salt in a large serving bowl. If not obviously juicy, crush lightly with a potato masher. Add the olive oil and ¾ cup of the torn basil leaves, tossing well. Add the garlic, red pepper flakes, and olives and season to taste. Leave at room temperature for 1 to 2 hours. (Keep in mind, the chile will get hotter as it sits, so add with caution.)

When ready to serve, bring a large pot of salted water to a boil over high heat. Add the spaghetti and cook until al dente according to the package instructions. Drain well and transfer to the bowl of the tomato mixture, tossing well to combine. Garnish with the remaining ¼ cup of torn basil and a sprinkle of flaky salt. Taste and add more red pepper flakes if desired and serve immediately.

Variation

If you want to serve this at room temperature, cook the pasta, drain well, and toss with 1 tablespoon of extra-virgin olive oil. Let cool to room temperature. When ready to serve, toss the room-temperature pasta with the sauce. If desired, add a couple handfuls of fresh mozzarella (preferably buffalo) cut into ½-inch pieces.

NOTE: *In a pinch, Kalamata olives will be fine. I don't use them personally because they have a retro '70s taste to me.*

Fresh Fettuccine
with Yogurt, Caramelized Onions,
and Tender Herbs

SERVES 4 TO 6

Light cream sauces provide an ideal backdrop to showcase the breezy-fresh flavors of tender herbs. This version is even lighter, as it relies simply on tart whole-milk yogurt instead of the richness of heavy cream. The thickened yogurt's gentle tang goes particularly well with the sweetness of the caramelized onions and the nutty pecorino romano, and it gets wonderfully saucelike when tossed with ribbons of fettuccine. Be sure to plan at least a day ahead to give the yogurt time to drain in the refrigerator overnight.

2 cups plain whole-milk yogurt or Greek yogurt (such as Nancy's brand)

5 tablespoons extra-virgin olive oil, plus more for drizzling

3 large onions, halved and sliced thinly

Sea salt and freshly ground black pepper

¼ cup broth or water

1 pound fresh fettuccine (see Basic Fresh Pasta, page 183)

2 cups tightly packed tender fresh herbs, chopped (a mixture of flat-leaf parsley, basil, chervil, fennel fronds, and/or chives)

1 cup grated pecorino romano

Fresh lemon juice or lemon agrumato, to taste

The day before: Fold a large piece of cheesecloth in half, then in half again. Spoon the yogurt into the center. Tie together the ends that are diagonally across from each other to make a bundle. Insert the handle of a long wooden spoon through the knot. Set the spoon across a large bowl, suspending the bundle and allowing it to drain. Refrigerate for 8 hours or overnight.

The day of: Remove the yogurt from the refrigerator (it should be quite thick). Discard the liquid in the bowl (or use it in a smoothie). Allow the yogurt to sit until it comes to room temperature.

Heat the oil in a large skillet over medium heat. Add the onion slices, season with salt and pepper, and sauté, stirring often, until the onions are creamy-soft and caramelized to a golden brown, 30 to 40 minutes, lowering the heat if the onions darken too quickly. Deglaze the pan with broth or water, and cook just until the liquid evaporates.

Meanwhile, cook the pasta in a large pot of salted water until just al dente, about 2 minutes. Scoop out and reserve 1 cup of pasta water before draining.

Place the yogurt in a large bowl and whisk in ½ cup of the hot pasta water. Add the drained pasta and toss. Fold in the caramelized onions and herbs. Add more pasta water if necessary to achieve a saucy consistency. Transfer the pasta to a large, warm serving bowl or divide among plates. Drizzle with olive oil, sprinkle with the cheese, and add a squeeze of lemon and pepper to taste.

Fennel Alfredo Pasta

SERVES 4 TO 6

● ●

This sauce is inspired by one my Tuscan friend Paolo Calamai made at his late and much-beloved Burrasca restaurant in Portland. Tuscans revere fennel, and in the true Italian tradition of wasting nothing, this recipe uses parts of the fennel that typically get thrown away. Although Alfredo sauce seems old school and easy to dismiss, when properly made with the best-quality butter, Parmesan, and cream (and no gloppy thickeners), it is a silky, timeless classic. Three forms of fennel—fresh, seeds, and distilled into Pernod—add a freshness to the luxe sauce that makes it ideal for summer.

One 12- to 14-ounce fennel bulb

1 cup whole milk

1 cup half-and-half

2 tablespoons Pernod (optional)

4 tablespoons (½ stick) unsalted butter

1 leek (white and light green part only), chopped finely

Sea salt

1 teaspoon fennel seeds, toasted and ground

Zest of 1 lemon

Freshly ground black pepper

One 8.8-ounce package dried pappardelle (the kind that comes in nests) or 1 pound fresh (see Basic Fresh Pasta, page 183)

1 cup finely grated Parmigiano-Reggiano, plus more for garnish

Freshly squeezed lemon juice for garnish (optional)

Remove the stalks, fronds and hard outside layers of the fennel bulb (save a few fronds for garnish) and roughly chop the bulb until you have about 2 cups of chopped fennel. Finely chop the remaining bulb and set aside.

Combine the roughly chopped fennel with the milk and half-and-half in a medium, heavy-bottomed saucepan over medium-high heat. Bring almost to a boil (the milk will be steaming with a few tiny bubbles around the edge of the pot). Lower the heat to low, cover, and gently cook until the fennel is completely tender, 40 to 45 minutes. Remove from the heat and allow to steep for 20 minutes.

Puree the fennel mixture in a blender until very smooth. Pass through a fine-mesh sieve set over a bowl, pressing on the solids. Discard the solids. You should have about 1½ cups of fennel cream. Stir in the Pernod, if desired, and set aside. This fennel cream can be made a day in advance and refrigerated.

Melt the butter in a large sauté pan over low heat. Add the finely chopped fennel and leek, season with a generous pinch of salt, and cook, stirring occasionally, until very soft, translucent, and beginning to break down, about 30 minutes. Keep an eye on the heat; you don't want the vegetables to get any color. Add the toasted ground fennel seeds and pour in the fennel cream. Gently heat, stirring, until the mixture is hot but not boiling. Remove from the heat, mix in the lemon zest, and season to taste with salt and pepper.

Meanwhile, boil the pasta in a large pot of salted water until al dente according to the package instructions (or about 2 minutes if using fresh pasta). Drain, saving 1 cup of the pasta water. Add the pasta to the fennel cream. Allow to heat through, stirring to coat the pasta and adding pasta water, if needed, to thin it out. Fold in the cheese.

Divide the pasta among bowls and garnish with fennel fronds. Top with more grated cheese and a squeeze of lemon juice, if desired.

Spaghettini with Garlic, Clams, and Bottarga

SERVES 4

You'll find lidos all along the coasts of Italy—private beaches with bright clusters of matching beach umbrellas and lounge chairs you can rent for an entire day of languorous sun-worshipping, surf-bobbing, and people-watching, fortified by a steady stream of spritzes delivered by waitstaff of the attached restaurant. Spending a summer day like this is one of my favorite things to do in Italy, and the best part is when you get hungry, you can walk over to the restaurant in your swimsuit and tuck into a bowl of spaghettini and clams with your toes in the sand and the water lapping just steps away. That's why, for me, this dish will always taste like the very essence of an Italian summer.

Spaghettini (often called "thin spaghetti" in the States) is the ideal shape for seafood sauces because it's thinner than spaghetti but not as hard to properly cook as angel hair, and it readily soaks up the delicate flavor of the sauce.

As for the clams, opt for small ones so that you'll have a lot, meaning a couple of clams in each bite. I do take an extra step to ensure all grit is removed from the clams; the grit is totally natural but sure would distract from the final texture of the dish.

2½ pounds small Manila clams

¼ cup extra-virgin olive oil

4 garlic cloves, sliced thinly

¼ cup chopped fresh flat-leaf parsley leaves, plus more for garnish

½ to 1 teaspoon red pepper flakes or ½ fresh red chile, cored, seeded, and chopped finely; or more to taste

1 pint cherry tomatoes, cut in half (optional)

⅓ cup white wine

12 ounces dried spaghettini (aka thin spaghetti)

Sea salt

2 tablespoons unsalted butter or extra-virgin olive oil (optional)

2 tablespoons finely grated Parmigiano-Reggiano (optional; see Note)

1½ ounces grated bottarga for garnish (see page xv; optional)

continues

Line a strainer with a clean floursack dish towel or two layers of cheesecloth and dampen it lightly. Set the strainer over a small bowl.

Soak the clams in cold water for 30 minutes. Drain, rinse well, and discard any that feel light or aren't tightly closed.

Put the clams in a 14-inch straight-sided sauté pan over high heat and cover the pan. Cook until the clams open, shaking the pan vigorously every few seconds (kind of as if you're making popcorn). Monitor the clams' progress, and when they open, transfer them to a bowl. If they're small, which is preferable, they might all open at the same time, so move fast! The clams should take only 3 or 4 minutes, but give any stubborn ones an extra minute or two; if they refuse to open, toss them out.

Remove the clams from their shells and place in a little bowl while capturing all their liquid in the original bowl. Discard the shells. Pour the clam liquid from both the sauté pan and the bowl through the cheesecloth-lined strainer to catch any grit. Gently dip the clams in the clam liquid to rinse them of any remaining grit and strain the liquid again. Combine the clams and strained liquid in a bowl. (Note that this process may sound complicated, but it will ensure all grit is removed and will make sense once you start cooking this dish.)

Rinse and dry the clam-cooking sauté pan and heat the olive oil in it over medium heat. Add the garlic and cook, stirring, for 1 minute, monitoring the heat to keep the garlic from browning. Add the parsley and red pepper flakes. If using tomatoes, add them and stir for about another minute to soften them slightly. Add the white wine and simmer until slightly reduced, 1 to 2 minutes. Remove from the heat.

Cook the spaghettini in boiling salted water until still very al dente, about 5 minutes. Drain, reserving some pasta water. Add the pasta to the sauté pan and return to medium heat. Strain the clam juice into the pasta (leaving the clams behind). Cook over medium heat until the juices coat the pasta. The sauce can be enriched by tossing with butter or olive oil and Parmesan. Add the cooked clams and toss. Add a little of the reserved pasta water if the mixture seems dry.

Pile the pasta and clams into wide bowls, making sure everyone gets their share of clams, and garnish with more parsley and the bottarga (if using). Serve immediately.

❮ ❮

NOTE: *Adding Parmesan to seafood pasta is definitely not traditional in Italy, but it is delicious. Don't be a slave to tradition. If you like Parm, add it! As an Italian winemaker once told me: "In Italy, all rules are written in pencil and every Italian is born with an eraser."*

Spaghettini with Clams, Zucchini, and Zucchini Blossoms

SERVES 4

● ●

Delicate spaghettini forms the perfect backdrop for briny little clams steamed in white wine and young, tender zucchini showered with their luscious blossoms. It's worth finding space in your yard for a zucchini plant just to be able to have an endless supply of blossoms for this lovely summertime dish. But if you can't find squash blossoms, don't stress. This dish is still wonderful without them.

1 pound Manila clams in shell

4 small, firm zucchini (preferably with their blossoms)

4 zucchini blossoms (for a total of 8 blossoms; optional)

⅓ cup extra-virgin olive oil, plus more for drizzling

2 small red spring onions, halved and sliced thinly

Sea salt

4 garlic cloves, thinly sliced

Pinch of red pepper flakes, or more to taste

12 ounces dried spaghettini (aka thin spaghetti)

⅓ cup dry white wine

12 fresh basil leaves

¼ cup coarsely chopped fresh flat-leaf parsley leaves

Soak the clams in cold water for 30 minutes. Drain, rinse well, and discard any that feel light or aren't tightly closed. Cut the zucchini in half lengthwise, then cut crosswise into thin half-moons. Reserve the zucchini blossoms until serving time.

Heat the olive oil in a large sauté pan (one that has a lid) over medium-high heat. Add the sliced spring onions and season with salt. Sauté until softened, about 4 minutes. Add the garlic and pepper flakes; sauté for about 1 minute. Add the zucchini, season with salt, and sauté until just beginning to soften, about 3 minutes.

Cook the spaghettini in boiling salted water until it is still very al dente, about 5 minutes. Drain, reserving ½ cup of the pasta water.

While the pasta cooks, add the clams to the zucchini, stir for a minute, then add the wine, cover, and steam until the clams open.

Add the drained pasta to the zucchini and clams. Toss together over medium heat for 1 to 2 minutes, adding the reserved pasta water, as needed, to make a loose but not watery sauce. Tear the zucchini blossoms and basil and add to the pan along with the parsley. Serve immediately with a generous drizzle of extra-virgin olive oil and more pepper flakes to taste.

Spaghettini with Prawns

SERVES 4

This is one of those easy-to-throw-together pastas that everyone should have in their repertoire, the kind of recipe you can make on the spur of the moment after a big day out at the beach. Because it's so elemental, the ingredients really count. Look for Gulf shrimp or prawns—the bigger the better—which will be wonderfully meaty and sweet. And use fresh, young garlic, even green garlic if you can find it, for a milder and more pleasant flavor. It's more than likely you already have most of the ingredients on hand. If you keep a bag of shrimp in the freezer, you can have this herby, garlicky tangle of noodles kissed with lemon on the table in minutes.

1 pound colossal (10 to 12 per pound) raw shrimp or prawns

½ cup extra-virgin olive oil , plus more for drizzling

½ bunch scallions, white and light green parts only, minced

3 large young garlic cloves, minced

½ teaspoon red pepper flakes, or ½ fresh red chile, seeded and chopped finely

Sea salt

10 ounces dried spaghettini (aka thin spaghetti)

⅓ cup chopped fresh flat-leaf parsley leaves

Squeeze of fresh lemon juice

Grated bottarga for garnish (see page xv; optional)

GCBC (Garlic Chile Bread Crumbs) for garnish (page 168; optional)

Peel and devein the shrimp, then cut in half lengthwise.

Heat the olive oil in a large sauté pan over medium-high heat. Add the scallions, garlic, and red pepper flakes; sauté for about 1 minute. Add the shrimp and sauté, stirring, until just barely cooked through, about 3 minutes. Remove from the heat and season with salt.

Cook the pasta in boiling salted water until al dente, about 5 minutes. Drain, reserving ½ cup of the pasta water. Toss the pasta with the shrimp in the sauté pan over medium heat for 1 to 2 minutes, adding the reserved pasta water as needed to make a loose but not watery sauce. Add the parsley and a squeeze of lemon to taste. Serve immediately, drizzled with more olive oil and garnished with bottarga (if using) and bread crumbs (if using).

Pici all'Aglione

SERVES 4 TO 6

Pici (sounds like "peachy") are rustic, hand-rolled noodles originally from the Tuscan city of Siena. Traditionally made with just flour and water, they require no special tools or pasta machine to make, just a willingness to tap into your Play-Doh–loving child within. That's why this is the best pasta shape for beginners and kids, or to trot out when you're vacationing at a beach house with a scarcity of kitchen tools. Named for a special variety of Tuscan garlic, the simple and similarly rustic tomato sauce is a classic accompaniment. Don't be afraid to make this even if you're serving only two—it doesn't require that much effort and the dough divides in half easily.

PICI DOUGH

7 ounces (200 g) all-purpose flour

7 ounces (200 g) semola rimacinata flour (see page xx), plus more for dusting

7 fluid ounces (200 g) lukewarm water

SUGO ALL'AGLIONE

⅓ cup plus 1 tablespoon extra-virgin olive oil

12 small garlic cloves, peeled and lightly crushed

One 28-ounce can whole peeled San Marzano tomatoes

Sea salt

½ teaspoon red pepper flakes

TO MAKE THE PICI DOUGH

Mix the flours together in a bowl. Make a well in the center and add the water. With a fork, mix well until the flour pulls away from the sides of the bowl. Empty the dough onto a clean work surface (preferably wooden, such as a cutting board) and knead until smooth, 10 to 12 minutes.

Form into a ball, shape into a disk, and cover with a bowl. Let rest for 30 minutes or wrap in plastic wrap and refrigerate overnight.

Divide the pasta dough into quarters. Dust the work surface with semola flour. Dust a baking sheet generously with semola flour and set it nearby.

Working with one quarter at a time and keeping the rest loosely covered with a towel or plastic wrap, use a rolling pin to roll the dough into a smooth rectangle about ¼ inch thick. Cut the rectangle into ¼-inch-wide strips. Using your palms, roll each strip out into a thin, spaghetti-like rope, starting in the center and working your way outward. (The ropes should be 8 to 10 inches long. The squigglyness of the noodles is its charm; just try to keep the width to ¼ inch and consistent for even cooking.) Place on the prepared baking sheet, sprinkling with a little more semola to keep it from sticking, and repeat with the rest of the dough.

TO MAKE THE SUGO ALL'AGLIONE

Heat the oil and garlic cloves in a large sauté pan or Dutch oven over medium heat. When the garlic just begins to sizzle, reduce the heat to low and cook gently, turning occasionally, until golden on all sides, watching the heat level to keep the garlic from burning.

Add the tomatoes and their juices, crushing the tomatoes with your hands as you add them to the pan. Season with a generous pinch of salt and the red pepper flakes. Cook over low heat, stirring often, until the mixture thickens and the oil floats to the surface of the sauce, 15 to 30 minutes (this can go fast or slow depending on how low your stove's setting is). Mash the garlic with a fork or potato masher and incorporate into the sauce. Season with more salt to taste. Keep warm.

TO FINISH

Cook the pici in a large pot of boiling salted water until al dente, 3 to 5 minutes. Scoop out ½ cup of the pasta water and reserve. Drain the pici and add to the tomato sauce. Cook over low heat, tossing, until evenly coated, adding a few splashes of pasta water, if necessary, to loosen the sauce. Divide among bowls and serve.

Shrimp Ravioli in Brodo

SERVES 6 TO 8

Some recipes are less about cooking and more about crafting. They're about seeing the kitchen as a workshop where you can spend a slow afternoon, creating things with your hands. This lovely dish from Nostrana executive chef Brian Murphy is one of those recipes. And when you're done grinding and rolling and shaping, you'll have about five dozen tender little pasta pockets filled with shrimp and herbs that ingeniously poach in butter as they cook. They're wonderfully luxurious without being heavy, especially when served in a light, shrimp-scented broth, and are the perfect backdrop of any number of fresh, tender herbs, such as anise-tinged chervil or tarragon, grassy parsley, and sweet-musky marjoram. You'd be wise to double the recipe and tuck some ravioli and brodo (broth) in the freezer for another day.

SHRIMP FILLING
1½ pounds whole, head-on, raw shrimp

12 tablespoons (1 stick plus 4 tablespoons) unsalted butter, cut into ½-inch cubes, frozen

1 to 2 tablespoons chopped fresh chives or other tender herbs (such as chervil, parsley, tarragon, or marjoram)

Sea salt and freshly ground black pepper

SHRIMP BRODO
1 tablespoon extra-virgin olive oil

1 tablespoon unsalted butter

Raw shrimp shells and heads from 1 pound of shrimp

1 tablespoon tomato paste

½ celery rib, chopped roughly

¼ carrot, chopped roughly

¼ large yellow onion, chopped roughly

¼ bulb fennel, chopped roughly

1 bay leaf

½ cup white wine

2 cups light chicken or fish broth

Water, as needed

Sea salt

ASSEMBLY
1 pound fresh pasta (see Basic Fresh Pasta, page 183)

Semola rimacinata flour (see page xx) for dusting

Garnish: 2 tablespoons chopped fresh chives, halved cherry tomatoes, and/ or blanched corn kernels

continues

TO MAKE THE SHRIMP FILLING

Remove the heads and shells from the shrimp and reserve for the brodo. Devein the shrimp and place in a large bowl. Toss in the butter cubes and chives. Season generously with salt and pepper. Freeze the mixture for 30 minutes to firm up before passing through the grinder.

Set up a meat grinder with a ¼-inch grinder plate or a food mill with a medium- or large-holed grating disk. Pass the mixture through the grinder according to the manufacturer's instructions. (You can grind bigger or smaller for a chunkier or smoother filling.) Gently fold the ground mixture together until evenly mixed, but do not overmix or it will bind too tightly together.

Cover and refrigerate until ready to use. The filling can be made 3 days ahead and refrigerated, or frozen for 3 months. Defrost overnight in the refrigerator before using.

TO MAKE THE SHRIMP BRODO

Heat the oil and butter in a large stockpot over medium heat (choose a pot large enough to fit about twice the volume of the shrimp shells). Add the shrimp shells and heads and stir to lightly toast but not brown, 5 minutes. Add the tomato paste and stir to coat the shells. Add the celery, carrot, onion, fennel, and bay leaf. Sauté, stirring constantly so nothing browns, until the vegetables barely start to soften, 7 minutes.

Add the wine and briefly remove from the heat, stirring to scrape up anything stuck to the bottom of the pot. Return to heat and add the broth and just enough water to just cover the shells. Season lightly with salt. Bring the mixture to a boil and then lower the heat to a bare simmer.

Simmer for 45 minutes, stirring occasionally, mashing the shrimp shells and heads against the bottom and side of the pot to release more flavor.

Pass the brodo through a fine-mesh sieve, squeezing out as much flavor from the shells as possible. The brodo can be made 3 days ahead and refrigerated, or frozen for up to 3 months.

TO ASSEMBLE

Divide the pasta dough into quarters. Working with one quarter at a time and keeping the rest covered with plastic wrap, roll out the dough on a pasta machine to about ¹⁄₁₆ of an inch (usually the last setting), dusting with semola flour as necessary to keep from sticking. As you pass the sheet of dough through each consecutively smaller setting, make sure it remains as wide as the roller.

Lay the sheet on a clean work surface dusted with semola flour and cut in half to create two sheets of equal length. Fold the first sheet along its midline to make a light crease and then reopen it. Drop heaping teaspoons of filling onto one side of the creased pasta sheet, spacing them ½ inch apart. Use a pastry brush to lightly brush water along the edges of the sheet and between each dollop of filling. Fold over the other half of the sheet and press around each dollop, from the crease to the outer edge, to remove as much air as possible and seal pasta around the filling. Use a pizza cutter, fluted wheel cutter, or sharp knife to trim the edges and cut between each mound of filling.

Arrange the ravioli, not touching, on a baking sheet lined with parchment paper and dusted with semola flour. Cover with a damp towel. Repeat with the remaining dough and filling. The ravioli can be frozen on the baking sheet until hard, then transferred to freezer bags. They will keep, frozen, for 3 months.

TO SERVE

Bring a large pot of salted water to a gentle rolling boil. In a separate pot, heat the strained brodo until just barely simmering.

Working in batches of about 10, cook the ravioli in the boiling water, lowering the heat as needed so they boil gently and don't get beat up, until they float to the surface and are no longer stiff, about 3 minutes. Remove with a slotted spoon and transfer to the warm brodo. Divide the ravioli and brodo among bowls, garnish as desired, and serve.

My Dinner with Marcella

Back in 1998, I was cooking at Genoa and already had two decades under my belt as a Marcella Hazan megafan. Her landmark cookbook, *Essentials of Classic Italian Cooking*, was my North Star in the kitchen. But she had a new book, *Marcella Cucina*, and her book tour took her to Portland and a guest spot on a public radio cooking show hosted by June Reznikoff, one of the original sous chefs at Genoa. Before the interview, June had invited Marcella and her husband, Victor, who always traveled with her, to dine at Genoa, but they firmly passed. "We don't eat Italian food in America," they said. Then, I got a call in the afternoon while prepping for that night's service. It was Victor. "We were very impressed by the interviewer," he said. "Can we still come to dinner?"

To say I was thrilled to cook for my hero is a massive understatement. Marcella influenced so much of what we did—even that night's menu featured one of her recipes. I was both honored and more than a little terrified. They came, they ate, and Marcella was sufficiently impressed to assume the chef was an Italian. She was so surprised to learn that the chef was actually a 42-year-old from North Carolina that she asked to meet me. I came out of the kitchen, practically shaking with nervous excitement, and found her enjoying a whiskey and cigarette in the sitting room in the back of the restaurant. Within minutes, she was inviting me to study with her in Venice. "I'm retiring, and I'll make space in my next class," she told me. It was an offer I could not and would not refuse.

Later that year, I traveled to Italy for the weeklong class, the second-to-last before she'd retire full time to Florida. My classmates were all rich and famous people of some sort, and then there was me, the only professional chef. But cooking alongside fashion designers and moguls was nothing compared to learning at the hands of Marcella herself. That week opened my world to so many things—especially to how gnocchi were supposed to taste. I never knew they could be so light! Now, I'm a gnocchi evangelist on a mission to teach everyone how to make gnocchi like Marcella.

Potato Gnocchi

SERVES 4

●●●●●●● ●● ●●● ●● ● ●●●●●●●● ● ●● ● ●● ●● ●● ●●●●●●● ●●● ●● ● ●●● ●● ● ●●●●●

You've probably cooked shelf-stable gnocchi from the supermarket—chewy, firm dump-lings that sink to the bottom of your stomach like lead balloons. If that's your prefer-ence, this is not the recipe for you. Actually, let me rephrase that: Try this recipe, but understand that the supermarket option will likely never bring you the same joy again. The best gnocchi are pillowy and light, magically straddling the line between firm and falling apart, something I learned from the late, great Marcella Hazan herself. Achieving this ethereal texture requires avoiding sog-inducing activities (choose a slightly waxy potato, don't poke too much during cooking, boil the gnocchi in small batches so the water returns to a simmer faster). It's also important to start with the minimum amount of flour you think you might need, then gradually add more just until the dough is soft, pliant, and smooth but not sticky.

If serving these for a dinner party, try tossing some in tomato sauce, some in pesto, and some with butter and sage, then plate up all three side by side as an edible ode to the Italian flag.

1½ pounds Yellow Finn or Yukon Gold potatoes (not newly dug), unpeeled, preferably all the same size

¾ to 1¼ cups (90 to 150 g) all-purpose flour

Flaky sea salt

Marcella Hazan's Tomato-Butter Sauce (page 182), or Basil Pesto (page 175) for serving

1 cup finely grated Parmigiano-Reggiano for garnish

Place the potatoes in a large pot and cover with water by a couple of inches. Bring to a boil over high heat, lower the heat to a steady simmer, and cook until tender, about 20 minutes once the water starts to boil. Choose one sacrificial potato to test with a wooden skewer; it should slide in and out easily. (Avoid testing too many times or the potato may become waterlogged.) When the potatoes are cooked, drain and peel as soon as you can handle them but while still hot (it will be much easier that way).

Press the potatoes through a potato ricer directly onto a clean work surface. Alternatively, use a potato masher and mash as thoroughly as possible, then refine the texture even more by mashing with a fork.

continues

Sprinkle the flour (start with the smaller amount) onto the potatoes and toss together, sifting through your fingers, until well incorporated. Begin kneading the dough, adding a little more flour as needed if the dough seems too soft, until the dough is smooth, soft, and not sticky (see "Gnocchi Know-How"). Cover with a clean towel to keep the mixture warm while you form the gnocchi.

Bring a small pot of water to a boil for testing the gnocchi when shaping.

Dust a smooth, wooden work surface with flour. Pinch off a handful of dough and roll it into a ¾-inch-thick log. Cut crosswise into ¾-inch lengths. Using your thumb, press each piece on a gnocchi paddle or the tines of a fork to create grooves on one side and an indentation on the other. Drop a few gnocchi into the boiling water. If they start to fall apart, knead a little more flour into the dough. If not, proceed to shape gnocchi from the remaining dough. The gnocchi can be shaped up to 4 hours ahead and kept covered by a towel (see "Gnocchi Know-How").

Place a serving platter in a warm spot near the stove or inside a very low oven and spread with a bit of your preferred sauce, reheated if necessary, so it's ready to combine with the gnocchi, which will be cooked in batches.

Fill a wide shallow pot (such as a Dutch oven) with water, bring to a boil, and salt well. Lower heat to a steady simmer. Drop in the gnocchi in batches of one-third to one-half of the recipe (adding too many at once can lower the temperature of the water too much and slow down the cooking process, resulting in waterlogged dumplings). Adjust the heat as necessary to maintain a steady simmer, not a full boil. When they float to the surface, let them cook for 10 to 15 seconds longer, then transfer with a large slotted spoon to the serving platter. Repeat with the remaining gnocchi. Each time you scoop out a new batch, drain thoroughly, add to the platter, add a bit more sauce, and toss very gently with a flexible spatula. Before you discard the cooking water, scoop out about a cup to use for adjusting the final consistency of your sauce.

Gently toss the gnocchi with the remaining sauce, just enough to coat well. Thin out with a few drops of the cooking water, if necessary. Garnish with Parmesan and serve more at the table.

Gnocchi Know-How

Gnocchi success is all in the details.

PERFECT POTATOES: I prefer medium-starch potatoes, such as Yellow Finn or Yukon Gold, because the flavor is quite potato-y but they don't contain a lot of water. Russets are low moisture and will work, too, but avoid red potatoes or any other variety known for having a high water content. The extra moisture will interact with the flour in the dough and create more gluten and toughness in the final gnocchi. And, although it pains me to say it, don't use fresh, new potatoes from the farmers' market because they have a high water content, too. Try to select potatoes that are all the same size so they'll cook at the same rate.

ADD FLOUR WITH CAUTION: The trick to knowing how much flour to use is to be one with the dough. Don't get hung up on precise measurements. Instead, let your senses and your instincts guide you. You have to be brave enough to stop adding flour at just the right point so as not to overwork the dough. If you poke it, it should be soft enough to leave an imprint. But you have to be generous enough that the dough isn't tacky and the dumplings will hold together when boiled. It's better to err on the side of using less flour; you can test the gnocchi when shaping and add more flour, if necessary. Keep in mind that if it's humid or rainy, you might need to use more flour.

SKIP THE EGG: Sure, adding an egg helps the dough hold together, but it also makes the gnocchi tougher. Marcella Hazan told me some traditional Italian restaurants might use an egg because they're making batches of 30 servings, but even then, they'd use only one.

MAKE-AHEAD TIPS: Gnocchi can start to get soft if they sit for more than a couple of hours, so cook them relatively soon after shaping. You can shape them up 4 hours ahead of cooking as long as the environment isn't too humid, but don't wait that long if it's a muggy day. Don't try to freeze gnocchi, as they will get mealy and fall apart.

BONUS FUN FACT: Did you know Thursdays are for gnocchi? Traditionally, in Rome, gnocchi are made on Thursdays, as it's supposed to be a filling dish before you have a fast day on Friday. That's what inspired our Giovedì Gnocchi tradition at Nostrana, when we take pasta off the menu each Thursday and serve only gnocchi.

Salt and Herb Focaccia
WITH VARIATIONS
MAKES ONE 9-BY-13-INCH PAN; 12 PIECES

❘❘❘

In Italian restaurants, bread baskets aren't a preamble to dinner. They're intended for guests to enjoy along with their meal, even if brought out ahead of time. Focaccia, however, is an exception to the rule. Unless used in a sandwich or as a street snack (merenda), it's always considered an appetizer, and that's how we treat it at Nostrana. We usually make six sheet pans of focaccia each day, and everyone looks forward to it as soon as they're seated. At once pillowy and chewy, herby and olive-oily, focaccia fresh from the oven is such a treat it'll spoil you for anything else. This makes a great appetizer for aperitivo hour, whether on its own or filled like a sandwich. It also makes a great pan pizza when topped with vegetables and sauce (tucking the vegetables under the sauce will keep them from getting dried out and leathery). If you have sourdough starter on hand, use it instead of yeast in the poolish for a more complex flavor.

POOLISH

9 ounces (260 g) high-gluten bread flour

9 ounces (260 g) cool water

⅛ teaspoon active dry yeast or 100 g sourdough starter

FOCACCIA

6 ounces (170 g) warm (80° to 90°F) water

¼ teaspoon active dry yeast

12 ounces (340 g) bread flour

6 tablespoons extra-virgin olive oil, plus more for drizzling

2 teaspoons sea salt

Flaky sea salt for sprinkling

1 tablespoon finely chopped fresh herbs, such as sage and rosemary

TO MAKE THE POOLISH

The day before: Mix together all poolish ingredients in a large bowl (preferably plastic because it's insulating) until no lumps remain. Cover with a clean dish towel and leave at room temperature to ferment overnight.

The next day: Check your poolish. It should be doubled in volume, with bubbles breaking on the surface. It should smell wheaty and yogurty. (If not using right away, refrigerate for up to 1 day.)

TO MAKE THE FOCACCIA

Add the warm water, yeast, bread flour, 2 tablespoons of the olive oil, and the salt to the poolish in the bowl. Mix until all the ingredients are combined and no dry bits remain. The dough should be evenly moist and stretchy. Cover and let rest for 10 minutes.

With moistened hands, lift up on one side of the dough, let it hang and stretch for a couple of seconds, then fold it over onto itself. Turn the bowl a quarter turn and repeat until you have lifted and folded the dough over four times. (Have faith! It will be wet and a bit messy at first, but it will come together as time goes on.) Cover and let rest for 30 minutes. Do this three more times (stretch, fold over, and turn until all four sides have been stretched, then let rest for 30 minutes). After stretching and folding over for the fourth time, cover and let the dough rise for 2 to 3 hours, until doubled in size and glossy.

Pour 2 tablespoons of the olive oil into a 9-by-13-inch baking dish and spread to coat. Scrape the dough into the baking dish, being careful not to deflate it. Gently flip it over to coat it in the oil.

Pick up the dough from the middle and allow the bottom half to hang and stretch to lengthen it a bit. Working on one corner at a time, gently pick up and pull the dough from underneath, stretching it from the middle into the corners of the pan. The goal is to coax the dough into covering the bottom and corners of the pan evenly and without tearing. Cover with plastic wrap and allow to rise for another 1 to 2 hours, until big bubbles are forming and the dough is very soft when poked. Alternatively, refrigerate and let it slowly rise overnight.

Preheat the oven to 450°F.

continues

Make indentations all over the surface of the dough (called docking) by using your fingertips to push down into the dough until you feel the bottom of the dish but not with such force as to make a hole. Spread the remaining 2 tablespoons of olive oil evenly across the surface. Sprinkle the surface evenly and generously with flaky salt. Then, evenly distribute the chopped herbs on top.

Dock the dough again. Let rest for 10 to 15 more minutes, until the dough is loose, bubbly, and wiggly when shaken. During this final rest, place an empty roasting pan in the oven below the center rack.

To bake, slide the focaccia pan onto the center rack and pour a cup of water into the hot roasting pan on the lower rack. Quickly close the oven door to trap the steam. Bake for 10 minutes, turn the focaccia pan front to back, and bake for 10 to 15 minutes more, until the top is firm and golden brown.

Remove from the oven and drizzle with more olive oil while still warm.

NOTE: For same-day focaccia, make a sponge instead of a poolish: In the morning, mix the same amount of flour and water called for in the poolish with a full teaspoon of the yeast called for in the recipe. Use warm water (80° to 90°F) rather than cool. Allow to sit for 2 to 3 hours before proceeding with the recipe, omitting any additional yeast when mixing the final dough.

Schiacciata con l'Uva

In this riff on a Tuscan classic, black or red grapes get baked into jammy pockets of sweetness, with fresh rosemary adding piney contrast.

2 cups small black or red grapes, stems
   removed

2 tablespoons sugar

1 tablespoon finely chopped fresh
   rosemary

Extra-virgin olive oil

Make the focaccia as directed, up to the point before it's sprinkled with herbs and flaky salt. Instead, scatter the grapes evenly over the dough. Sprinkle evenly with the sugar and rosemary. Continue with the recipe, docking the dough again, letting it rest, baking, and drizzling.

Focaccia with Caramelized Onions, Gorgonzola, and Anchovies

A deeply savory take layered with sweet onions, tangy cheese, and briny anchovies that can stand on its own as an appetizer.

1 tablespoon extra-virgin olive oil

1 tablespoon unsalted butter

2 large yellow onions, halved and sliced thinly

1 teaspoon chopped fresh thyme

¼ cup broth or water, or more as needed

2 ounces salt-packed anchovies, rinsed, soaked, and filleted (see page xiv)

6 ounces Gorgonzola cheese, crumbled

Extra-virgin olive oil

Heat the oil and butter in a large, heavy-bottomed sauté pan over medium heat. Add the onion slices and cook, stirring and scraping up the browned bits every 5 or 10 minutes, until they are deeply browned and caramelized, about 1 hour, reducing the heat to low once the onions soften to keep them from burning. Add the thyme, deglaze the pan with broth or water, and cook just until the liquid evaporates.

Make the focaccia as directed, up to the point before it's sprinkled with herbs and flaky salt. Instead, spread the caramelized onions evenly over the top. Tear the anchovies and arrange evenly over the onions. Evenly sprinkle the Gorgonzola crumbles over all. Continue with the recipe, docking the dough again, letting it rest, and baking. Focaccia loaded with toppings like this can take longer to cook. If it's soft and pale after 30 minutes, reduce heat to 400°F and bake 10 to 20 minutes more until the top feels firm. Drizzle with oil while still warm.

Margherita Pizza
WITH VARIATIONS
MAKES 6 PIZZAS (3 POUNDS OF DOUGH)

ϾϾ

There's never a time of year when pizza isn't welcome at the table, but I think summer is its prime time to shine. That's when you can cook it outdoors and give it a wisp of smoke from the grill, and top it with seasonal vegetables, such as zucchini, fresh herbs, tender arugula, and, really, anything else from the garden. Pizza is a favorite order at Nostrana, where you'll find most of our guests are unable to resist starting out their meal with a seasonal pie from our wood-fired oven. The chewy, flavorful dough took a thousand iterations to perfect, but it was worth it. There are an infinite number of ways to top it (the Sweet Italian Pork Sausage on page 138 would be phenomenal), but here are five of our greatest hits. Feel free to double the pizza dough and freeze it in 8-ounce balls to make future pizza parties even easier.

PIZZA DOUGH
23 ounces (655 g) warm (80° to 90°F) water

3 ounces (90 g) sourdough starter

19 ounces (545 g) white whole wheat flour, plus more for dusting

12 ounces (365 g) bread flour

3 teaspoons (18 g) salt

Pinch of diastatic malt powder (optional)

Semolina or semola rimacinata flour (see page xx) for dusting the peel

TOPPINGS
½ cup imported tomato passata or tomato sauce

3 ounces fresh mozzarella, sliced

10 fresh basil leaves, torn

Flavorful extra-virgin olive oil for drizzling

Optional additions: 2 to 3 anchovy fillets, cut in half lengthwise, and/or 1½ ounces baby arugula, tossed with a light drizzle of extra-virgin olive oil and flaky sea salt

TO MAKE THE PIZZA DOUGH
Whisk together the water and starter in a large plastic bowl until the starter dissolves. Add the flours, salt, and diastatic malt powder, if using. Mix for a few minutes, until a stiff dough forms and the ingredients are well combined. Cover the bowl with plastic wrap and rest at room temperature for 30 minutes. With moistened hands, lift up on one side of the dough, let it hang and stretch for a couple of seconds, then fold it over onto itself. Turn the bowl a quarter turn and repeat until you have lifted and folded the dough over four times. Cover

continues

and let rest for 30 minutes. Repeat the folding technique, then cover and refrigerate overnight or up to 24 hours to allow the dough to ferment slowly.

Remove the dough from the refrigerator. Turn out onto a clean, dry, lightly floured work surface and divide into six equal-size pieces about 8 ounces (275 grams) each. Shape each piece into a ball. Place the dough balls on a lightly floured baking sheet and cover loosely with plastic wrap or a clean dish towel. Allow to rise in a warm place for 4 to 6 hours, or until doubled in volume and somewhat puffy.

Alternatively, you can refrigerate the dough balls for up to 24 hours for slow rise, or freeze for longer storage. Allow to defrost overnight in the refrigerator. Let the dough stand at room temperature for 1 to 2 hours before stretching, topping, and baking.

TO ASSEMBLE

Preheat a pizza stone in a 500°F oven for 30 minutes or on a hot (500° to 550°F) grill prepared for indirect cooking.

Lightly dust a pizza peel with semolina or semola flour. Alternatively, use an upside-down rimmed baking sheet covered with parchment.

On a lightly floured work surface, gently stretch one dough ball into an 8- or 9-inch round. Pick the dough up at one edge, letting the bottom droop toward the counter, and rotate the dough through your fingers, inch by inch, letting gravity stretch it evenly as you move it around like a clock. Drape the dough over the backs of your hands and gently move them apart, letting the weight of the dough help to stretch it into a 12-inch round. Place on the floured pizza peel.

Use the back of a spoon to spread the tomato passata evenly over the shaped dough, leaving a ½-inch bare border. Arrange the fresh mozzarella evenly on top.

Shake the pizza peel to make sure the dough isn't sticking; if it is, lift up the troublesome areas and dust a little more semolina underneath. Quickly slide the pizza off the peel onto the preheated stone in the oven or grill. Cook (covered if on the grill) until the bottom is crisp and beginning to char and the cheese is melted, 8 to 12 minutes.

Use the pizza peel to slide the pizza off the pizza stone and onto a cutting board. Top with torn basil and drizzle with extra-virgin olive oil. Add anchovies and/or arugula, if desired. Cut into wedges and serve.

Marinara Pizza

A simple, cheese-free option that showcases elemental flavors of tomato sauce, slow-fermented dough, and good olive oil.

One 12-inch round of pizza dough on a
   lightly floured pizza peel

½ cup imported tomato passata or
   tomato sauce

1½ teaspoons dried Sicilian oregano

1 garlic clove, sliced very thinly

2 to 3 anchovy fillets, cut in half
   lengthwise (optional)

Flavorful extra-virgin olive oil for
   drizzling

Use the back of a spoon to spread the tomato passata evenly over the shaped dough, leaving a ½-inch bare border. Sprinkle evenly with the oregano and garlic.

Follow the baking instructions for the margherita pizza. Remove from the pizza stone and top with the anchovies, if using. Drizzle with olive oil. Cut into wedges and serve.

Funghi Verde Pizza
MAKES 1 PIZZA

● ●

Roasted wild mushrooms provide an earthy backdrop to creamy mozzarella, piquant pecorino, shaved garlic, and peppery arugula. A drizzle of lemon agrumato (olive oil pressed with citrus) at the end wakes up all of the flavors. In my opinion, this is best if enjoyed with a farm-fresh egg cooked on top.

5 ounces shiitake mushrooms, stems removed, caps quartered

3 ounces maitake mushrooms, torn into large pieces

Extra-virgin olive oil for tossing

Salt and freshly ground black pepper

One 8-ounce ball of pizza dough

2 garlic cloves, sliced very thinly

2 ounces fresh mozzarella, torn

1 large egg (optional)

½ ounce finely grated pecorino romano

Lemon agrumato for drizzling

1½ ounces arugula

Flaky sea salt

Preheat the oven to 425°F. Toss the mushrooms with just enough olive oil to lightly coat. Season with salt and pepper. Spread on a baking sheet and roast until tender and crispy at the edges, 20 to 25 minutes.

Shape the pizza dough into a 12-inch round and lay on a lightly floured pizza peel. Sprinkle the roasted mushrooms evenly over the shaped dough, leaving a ½-inch bare border. Sprinkle evenly with the sliced garlic. Arrange the mozzarella pieces on top. If desired, crack an egg into the middle of the pizza.

Follow the baking instructions for the margherita pizza. Remove from the pizza stone, sprinkle evenly with grated pecorino, drizzle with lemon agrumato, season with salt and pepper. Toss the arugula with a drizzle of olive oil and sprinkle with flaky sea salt. Pile the dressed arugula on the pizza. Cut into wedges and serve.

Granchio Pizza

MAKES 1 PIZZA

A rich base of crème fraîche gets topped with sweet Dungeness crab, smoky paprika butter, and fresh peppery arugula.

2 garlic cloves

1 teaspoon smoked paprika

⅛ teaspoon cayenne pepper

1 teaspoon fresh lemon juice

2 tablespoons melted unsalted butter

2 tablespoons crème fraîche

One 12-inch round of pizza dough on a lightly floured pizza peel

1 ounce provolone, grated on the large holes of a box grater

2 scallions, trimmed and sliced thinly

2 ounces Dungeness crabmeat, picked over to remove any shells

1 tablespoon finely chopped fresh chives

Sea salt and freshly ground black pepper

1 lemon wedge

Pound the garlic into a paste in a mortar and pestle. Mix in the smoked paprika, cayenne, lemon juice, and butter.

Use the back of a spoon to spread the crème fraîche evenly over the shaped dough, leaving a ½-inch bare border. Sprinkle with the provolone, scallions, and crabmeat. Drizzle with the paprika butter.

Follow the baking instructions for the margherita pizza. Remove from the oven, sprinkle with chives, season with salt and pepper, and squeeze the lemon wedge over all. Cut the pizza into wedges and serve.

Zucca Pizza

• •

For this fresh and summery pizza, tender zucchini mingles with a duo of melty cheeses and a sprinkle of garlic and onion.

1 garlic clove, very thinly sliced

1 ounce Raschera, grated (or any similar mild melty cheese, such as Muenster)

One 12-inch round of pizza dough on a lightly floured pizza peel

1 tablespoon olive oil, plus more for drizzling

1 small zucchini, sliced thinly

Sea salt

¼ small red onion, thinly sliced vertically

1 ounce plain goat cheese

⅛ teaspoon Espelette or Aleppo pepper, or more to taste

1 tablespoon finely chopped fresh chives

1 or 2 lemon wedges

Freshly ground black pepper

Scatter the sliced garlic and Raschera evenly over the shaped dough, leaving a ½-inch bare border. Drizzle with half of the olive oil.

In a medium bowl, drizzle the zucchini slices with the remaining olive oil, season with salt, and toss to coat. Arrange evenly in a single layer on top of the dough. Spread the red onion slices over the zucchini. Place 1½ teaspoon-size dollops of goat cheese evenly over the pizza. Sprinkle with the Espelette or Aleppo pepper.

Follow the baking instructions for the margherita pizza. Remove from the pizza stone, sprinkle with chives, squeeze a lemon wedge or two over all, season with salt and black pepper, and drizzle with olive oil. Cut into wedges and serve.

Zucchini Parmigiana

SERVES 4

Far easier than eggplant or chicken parmigiana but just as soul-satisfying, this cheesy casserole makes wonderful use of all the zucchini going gangbusters in your yard or at the farmers' market. Fresh mozzarella, a light tomato sauce, and a heap of basil keep this dish light on its feet, while a pre-oven stint on the grill gives the vegetables a welcome touch of smoky depth.

2 pounds zucchini, cut into ½-inch-thick rounds

1½ pounds sweet onions, sliced into ½-inch-thick rounds

¼ cup extra-virgin olive oil, plus more for brushing

Sea salt

Freshly ground black pepper

2½ cups Summery Tomato Sauce (page 180)

1 pound fresh mozzarella, drained, patted dry, and sliced

1 cup finely grated Parmigiano-Reggiano

6 basil sprigs, leaves torn

Prepare a grill for direct cooking over medium-high heat (400° to 450°F). Brush the cooking grates clean. Brush the zucchini and spring onion slices with oil on one side, sprinkle with salt and pepper, and arrange, oil side down, on the grates. Grill for 3 to 5 minutes, until grill marks appear. Brush the tops with oil, sprinkle with salt and pepper, and turn them over. Grill on the second side until grill marks appear, 2 to 3 minutes. Transfer to a platter and let cool.

Preheat the oven to 375°F. Coat an 8-by-8-inch baking dish with 1 tablespoon of the olive oil.

Spread ½ cup of tomato sauce in the baking dish. Add a layer of zucchini to cover the sauce. Top the zucchini with half of the spring onion slices. Spread about 1 cup tomato sauce evenly over the onions. Add half of the mozzarella slices, sprinkle with half of the Parmesan and half the basil. Repeat the layering once more: zucchini, spring onions, tomato sauce, mozzarella, Parmesan, and basil. Drizzle with the remaining 3 tablespoons of olive oil.

Bake in the upper third of the oven until golden on top and bubbling, 30 to 40 minutes. Remove from the oven and let cool for at least 15 minutes or to room temperature before serving.

Roasted Peppers in Crema

SERVES 4

❮ ❮

This dish, inspired by Mexican rajas con crema, makes a rich and versatile vegetarian entrée when served atop grilled or soft polenta. Our prep cooks would frequently make it for family meal tacos as an excuse to use the gorgeous poblano peppers grown by nearby 47th Avenue Farm. It quickly became a beloved staff favorite, and we decided it was just too good to keep for ourselves. It's not Italian, but adding fried polenta, fresh basil, and Parmesan brings it close enough. Although you can use other meaty peppers, even Italian frying peppers, the poblanos have a nutty bitterness and restrained heat that balances the richness of the dish.

1 pound poblano peppers (or other large, meaty peppers, such as Anaheim or bell)

¼ cup extra-virgin olive oil

1 small yellow or white onion, julienned

2 garlic cloves, minced

Sea salt

1 tablespoon tomato paste, or 1 Roma tomato, chopped coarsely

⅔ cup sour cream

⅓ cup heavy cream

Polenta (soft or grilled) for serving

Fresh basil for serving

Finely grated Parmigiano-Reggiano for serving

Prepare a grill for direct cooking over medium-high heat (400° to 450°F). Arrange the peppers on the cooking grate and grill until charred, about 10 minutes. Turn them and continue to grill until charred on all sides, about 10 more minutes total. The key is to not cook the flesh of the pepper too much while blistering the skin. Place the peppers in a clean paper bag and fold the top to seal, or place in a bowl and cover with plastic wrap. Let the peppers cool for about 20 minutes as the trapped steam loosens the skins.

Alternatively, preheat the broiler. Arrange the peppers on a baking sheet and broil until the surfaces are charred and wrinkled, about 6 minutes per side. Remove from the heat and cover the baking sheet tightly with foil to steam.

continues

When the peppers are cool enough to handle, use your fingers to peel off the charred skins. Remove the stems, cut in half, and remove the seeds. (Resist the urge to rinse them, as it removes a lot of flavor.) Cut the peeled peppers in half crosswise, then lengthwise into ½-inch-wide strips. You should have about 9 ounces of peppers.

Heat the olive oil in a 10-inch skillet over medium heat. Add the onion and cook until beginning to soften, about 5 minutes. Add the garlic and a pinch of salt, lower the heat to medium-low, and continue to cook until the onion is soft and translucent but not browning. Add the tomato paste and season with salt. If using chopped tomato, cook until completely soft. Add the pepper strips and simmer the mixture until soft and almost melted, about 10 minutes. If the mixture looks dry, add up to ¼ cup of water.

Add the sour cream and cream, and bring the mixture back to a simmer. Cook for a few minutes, or until thickened. Remove from the heat and season with salt to taste. Serve spooned on top of soft or grilled polenta. Garnish with fresh basil and grated Parmesan.

Roman Stuffed Tomatoes with Rice
(POMODORI AL RISO)
SERVES 4 AS MAIN DISH, 8 AS A SIDE DISH OR APPETIZER

Every sweltering summer in Rome, rice-stuffed tomatoes take center stage in the city's rotisserias and tavolas caldas (hot tables), where you can pick up premade meals and avoid having to turn on the oven at home. Cooked in the cool early hours of the day, they sit at room temperature until lunch or dinner time, the flavors melding and deepening as the hours tick on. Even if you don't need to bake these early to avoid the late-day heat, do it anyway. I'm a firm believer that the dish is best at room temperature or slightly warm. It might seem odd to add roasted potatoes to the pan, but it's a tradition born out of practicality—they help hold the tomatoes up!—and they make this dish a little more substantial, whether served alone with a fresh salad or alongside grilled meat or fish.

¾ cup uncooked Carnaroli or Arborio rice

8 firm but ripe medium tomatoes (about 3 inches in diameter)

Sea salt

¾ cup loosely packed fresh basil leaves, torn

¾ cup cubed fresh mozzarella

⅓ cup finely grated Parmigiano-Reggiano

2 anchovy fillets, chopped

1 garlic clove, minced finely

½ cup extra-virgin olive oil

Freshly ground black pepper

7 ounces Yukon Gold potatoes, peeled, cut into 1-inch-thick wedges

Preheat the oven to 375°F.

Bring a saucepan of water to a boil over high heat and salt generously. Add the rice and cook for 6 minutes; drain (it will still be firm).

Line a 9-by-13-inch baking dish with several layers of paper towels. Cut the top ½ inch off the tomatoes and reserve.

With a melon baller, hollow out the tomatoes and transfer the pulp and seeds to a food mill fitted with a medium or fine disk. Mill the pulp to remove the seeds, collecting the tomato pulp and its juices in a medium bowl and discarding the seeds. Alternatively, hand separate the tomato pulp from the gelatinous seeds, then chop the pulp coarsely and place

continues

in a medium bowl. Place the seeds in a fine-mesh sieve set over the bowl, press on them to extract any remaining juices into the bowl of pulp, then discard the seeds.

Sprinkle the inner sides of the hollowed-out tomatoes with salt and turn the tomatoes upside down in the prepared baking dish to drain for 10 minutes.

Add the parcooked rice, torn basil leaves, mozzarella, Parmesan, anchovies, garlic, and ¼ cup of the olive oil to the tomato pulp in the bowl. Season with salt and pepper to taste.

Discard the paper towels from the baking dish and lightly oil it. Arrange the tomato tops, cut side down, and space them evenly apart on the baking sheet (they will serve as a pedestal to stabilize the tomatoes). Loosely fill the tomatoes with the rice mixture, taking care not to overstuff or pack too densely. Set the filled tomatoes on the tomato tops.

Toss the potato wedges with 3 tablespoons of the olive oil and sprinkle with salt and pepper. Tuck the potatoes around the tomatoes to help hold them up. Drizzle everything with the remaining tablespoon of olive oil, or more if desired.

Cover the dish with foil and bake for 45 minutes, or until the tomatoes and rice are soft. Remove the foil and continue to bake until the potatoes are golden and cooked through, 20 to 25 minutes more. Remove from the oven and allow the tomatoes to cool until warm or room temperature before serving.

Summer Zucchini Risotto
WITH SAVORY FRUIT VARIATIONS
SERVES 4

Early-summer zucchini has a delicate, sweet flavor and firm texture that's wonderful in so many dishes. To celebrate its mild, vegetal sweetness, I love making risotto with it as a base and using water instead of broth so its flavor can shine. Other mild but high-quality ingredients complement it well, such as fresh extra-virgin olive oil, rich European-style butter, and the best Parmigiano-Reggiano you can find.

12 ounces small or medium zucchini

4 cups water, or 3 cups water plus 1 cup vegetable or light chicken broth

3 tablespoons extra-virgin olive oil

½ cup finely chopped onion (use fresh, early summer onions or scallions)

Sea salt

3 young garlic cloves, minced

1½ cups uncooked Carnaroli or Arborio rice

3 tablespoons white wine, fruity rosé, or Prosecco (see Note)

¾ cup finely grated Parmigiano-Reggiano, plus more for serving

3 tablespoons unsalted butter

Freshly ground black pepper

1 batch Salsa di Pomodoro (page 6), at room temperature

12 large fresh basil leaves, torn just before serving

Flavorful extra-virgin olive oil for drizzling

Place the zucchini in a bowl of cold or icy water and soak for 20 minutes (this will freshen and firm them). Drain, pat dry, and cut into ¼-inch dice.

Meanwhile, bring the water (or the water and broth mixture, if using) to a simmer in a medium saucepan over medium heat. Cover and keep hot.

While the water comes to a boil, heat the olive oil in a deep saucepan over medium heat. Add the onion, season with salt, and sauté until soft and translucent, about 10 minutes. Add the garlic and sauté for 2 minutes more, or until just starting to turn golden. Add the diced zucchini, season with salt, and sauté until the zucchini softens and wilts slightly, about 10 minutes.

Add the rice and sauté until the edges become translucent, about 3 minutes (don't let it burn). Add the wine and cook until evaporated, about 1 minute. Add a ladleful of the

continues

simmering liquid and cook, stirring constantly, until absorbed. Continue to add the liquid, one ladleful at a time, stirring continuously until it has almost completely evaporated (but the rice isn't sticking) before adding more. Continue for 18 to 20 minutes, until the rice is tender but still a little firm at the very center (al dente). It will continue to cook for at least 3 more minutes, so don't overcook. If you run out of the hot liquid before the rice has finished cooking, use a little more boiling water.

Remove the rice from the heat and add the Parmesan, butter, salt, and a generous amount of pepper. Stir vigorously with a wooden spoon for 1 minute.

Let the risotto rest for 3 minutes, then serve in warmed shallow bowls. Garnish each with a spoonful of salsa di pomodoro, a sprinkle of torn basil leaves, and a drizzle of your best extra-virgin olive oil. Pass more grated Parmesan at the table.

NOTE: *No one wants to open a bottle of white wine just for a few tablespoons. And yet you don't want to forgo it because wine adds acidity and the alcohol helps distribute flavors. Of course, you can simply plan to enjoy the rest of the bottle with your dinner. Or do what I often do: keep a bottle in the fridge that I continuously top off with leftover white wine, sparkly Prosecco, or fruity rosé, so I always have a smidge at the ready for cooking. The everlasting bottle isn't a new idea—I think I got it from an old cookbook about what popes eat—but it's brilliant nonetheless.*

Savory Fruit Risotto Variations
SERVES 4

Italians know fruits don't have to stay in the dessert lane. It's all in the way you cook them. Mostarda, the zesty condiment of candied fruit with a generous hit of mustard, is just one classic example. These summery risottos are another. By cooking the rice with onions, garlic, and light broth and generously adding salt, pepper, and umami-rich Parmesan, the sweetness of the fruit gets pulled into balance, resulting in light and bright risottos that still offer plenty of depth. Balance really is the key here: opt for light broths, or cut the broth with water so it doesn't overwhelm the delicate fruit flavor. By the same token, if the fruit is very sweet, as some of our Oregon strawberries can be, use less so that the savoriness can come through. It also helps to treat half the fruit as a vegetable, adding it early in the cooking process and saving the rest to add at the end, where it can provide more prominent bursts of flavor. For these variations, follow the main recipe with the following alterations, and skip the topping of salsa di pomodoro.

VARIATION #1
Strawberry and Basil Risotto

Use 4 cups of light chicken broth instead of water.

Omit the zucchini.

Cut 8 to 12 ounces of fresh strawberries into ½- to ¾-inch pieces (if the strawberries are completely ripe and sweet, 8 ounces is enough).

Add half of the strawberries to the pan when adding the first ladleful of broth. Add the remaining strawberries when the rice is almost done.

If the broth runs out before the rice is done cooking, use a little boiling water to finish (don't use more broth, or it could overwhelm the fruit flavor).

Season the risotto with a squeeze of lemon juice to taste.

To serve, omit the salsa di pomodoro. Garnish with a drizzle of balsamic tradizionale (the good stuff) along with the basil, Parmesan, and olive oil.

continues

Cantaloupe and Prosciutto Risotto

Use 4 cups of light chicken broth instead of water.

Omit the zucchini.

Use 2 cups of seeded and diced (½-inch) cantaloupe or other muskmelon. Add half to the pan when adding the first ladleful of broth.

Add 1 tablespoon of tomato paste halfway through cooking.

If the broth runs out before the rice is done cooking, use a little boiling water to finish (don't use more broth, or it could overwhelm the fruit flavor).

Add the remaining melon when the rice is almost done.

Season the risotto with a squeeze of lemon juice to taste.

To serve, omit the salsa di pomodoro. Garnish with fresh mint instead of basil, and eight paper-thin slices of prosciutto di Parma or di San Daniele, torn into pieces, along with the Parmesan and olive oil.

Risotto Done Right

Risotto is simple to make, but perfecting it requires attention to detail. You're aiming for a state called all'onda, which means "wave" and refers to its porridgelike consistency that flows and rolls when agitated. When spooned into a warm, shallow bowl, it should slowly spread out into a puddle. Here are the details to keep in mind:

THE RICE: Carnaroli, Arborio, and Vialone Nano are traditionally used in risotto for a reason—they're short-grain varieties with an abundance of amylopectin starch that breaks down with friction from stirring and heat, dissolving into the liquid to create a built-in creamy sauce. I opt for Carnaroli because it has a little more structure and resists getting mushy. In Venice, they use Vialone Nano, particularly for fish risottos, because it's a smaller grain with a more delicate quality that's suited to the fish.

THE POT: Use a tall, straight-sided pot, which will give you more surfaces to push the rice against and create friction that will release the starch every time you stir.

THE STIR: Yes, you must continuously add the liquid little by little. This produces the all-important friction that allows the rice to release the starches that create its creamy, velvety sauce, all while it cooks evenly.

THE TIMING: Once you start adding the liquid, Carnaroli should cook in 13 to 18 minutes. The only way to know it's done is to taste it, and frequently. Remove from the heat when the rice is just a few minutes away from being cooked all the way through—it will still have a tiny bit of firmness in the center of the grain—because the residual heat will finish the cooking process. Let it rest for 3 minutes before adding the butter and cheese to finish.

THE MANTECATURA: This is the term for vigorously beating cold butter and cheese into the risotto to emulsify them into the mixture and even incorporate a little air. It's the secret to the creamiest, dreamiest risotto. After beating, let the risotto rest for 3 minutes before serving.

THE SERVING BOWL: Ladle the risotto into warmed shallow bowls so it doesn't seize up and get gloppy from hitting a cold dish. Victor Hazan taught me that Italians eat it from the outside in, since it's cooler along the edges and allows the middle to stay warm.

Fish in a Venetian-Style Vinaigrette
(PESCE IN SAOR)

SERVES 6 AS AN APPETIZER, 4 AS MAIN COURSE

• •

Take a trip back in time through history's cookbooks and you'll find no shortage of recipes for making or using preserved fish. For something so abundant but so quick to spoil, finding ways to preserve it just makes a lot of sense. This recipe is my attempt to bring back the trend. On a hot summer day when you don't want to cook, you'll be thanking your past self for having this healthy, flavorful meal at the ready. It takes lightly fried fish fillets—nearly any variety will work—and blankets them in onions spiked with vinegar, honey, raisins, and pine nuts. The cooked fish fillets marinate in the mixture, so they'll keep for up to a week and get even more flavorful as the days go on. There are more elaborate versions in various parts of Italy—even landlocked areas where freshwater fish, such as eel, trout, and sturgeon, would be used—but I love the simplicity of this Venetian version from my friend Judy Witts Francini. Serve the fish alone, on crostini (see page 4) or Bruschetta (page 6), or on lightly dressed greens.

1½ pounds boneless, skinless fish fillets, such as halibut, rockfish, lingcod, sole, trout, mackerel, sardines, or swordfish

Sea salt and freshly ground black pepper

1 cup (120 g) all-purpose flour

Generous pinch of finely chopped red pepper flakes

Extra-virgin olive oil for frying

1 pound white onion or shallots, halved and sliced thinly

1 cup good-quality white wine vinegar or Champagne vinegar

½ cup water

2 bay leaves

3 tablespoons pine nuts, lightly toasted

3 tablespoons golden raisins

1 tablespoon honey, or to taste

Chopped fresh chives for garnish

High-quality extra-virgin olive oil for drizzling

Cut the fish diagonally into small pieces, 1½ to 2 ounces each. Pat dry with paper towels. Sprinkle with salt and pepper.

Place the flour in a shallow bowl and season with salt, black pepper, and the red pepper flakes. Dredge the fish in the seasoned flour and shake off the excess.

Heat ¼ inch of olive oil in a 12-inch skillet over medium-high heat until shimmering (about 350°F). Working in batches if necessary to avoid crowding the pan, fry the fish until lightly golden, about 3 minutes. Turn them and fry until golden, about 2 minutes more. Transfer to a paper towel–lined plate and repeat with the remaining fillets. Season with salt and black pepper.

Drain all but about 2 tablespoons of the oil. Return the skillet to medium heat and add the onion slices, Champagne vinegar, water, and bay leaves. Season with salt. Cook the onions slowly, tossing with tongs, until wilted and translucent, about 10 minutes. Stir in the pine nuts, raisins, and honey.

Spread about half of the onion mixture in a glass or ceramic baking dish. Add the fish, then spread with the remaining onion mixture. Cover and refrigerate overnight.

Bring the fish and onions to room temperature before serving. Garnish with a drizzle of extra-virgin olive oil and chopped chives.

Lemon-Marinated Fried Rockfish
(BRANZINO IN ACETO)

SERVES 6

Fried fish can often seem a bit heavy, but when it first gets a leisurely bath in a lemony marinade, it becomes deliciously bright and sassy. Any firm white fish will work with this recipe, and the double dip in flour ensures they cook up super crispy. I like to serve this with agliata, a creamy sauce thickened with bread and emboldened with grassy parsley. Akin to an herby aioli, the Florentine sauce has roots reaching all the way back to the 13th century. However, this version from longtime Nostrana head chef Brian Murphy—which makes about two cups—is a bit more modern, with artisan bread replacing the walnuts of antiquity. It's an incredible accompaniment to fried branzino, but it's just as good served with fried oysters, slathered on a chicken sandwich, or used as a dip for vegetables. Really, you can use it anywhere you'd use aioli.

LEMON-MARINATED FRIED ROCKFISH

3 pounds rockfish fillets, or any firm white fish, such as cod, lingcod, or sea bass

¼ cup plus 1 tablespoon freshly squeezed lemon juice

One 2-ounce can oil-packed anchovies, drained and gently rinsed

3 garlic cloves

2 tablespoons chopped fresh flat-leaf parsley leaves

2½ teaspoons dried Sicilian oregano

1 tablespoon dry mustard

Freshly ground black pepper

⅓ cup plus 1 tablespoon extra-virgin olive oil

3 large eggs

1½ cups (180 g) all-purpose flour

Sea salt

Avocado or grapeseed oil for frying

1½ lemons, cut into wedges, for serving

AGLIATA

1½ ounces day-old, crustless rustic bread or focaccia

2 tablespoons Champagne vinegar

2 tablespoons white wine

3 garlic cloves

½ cup fresh flat-leaf parsley

Sea salt

2 egg yolks

¾ cup neutral oil, such as avocado or grapeseed

¾ cup extra-virgin olive oil

Freshly ground black pepper

TO MAKE THE FISH

Remove any pin bones from the fish and cut into twelve 4-ounce portions. Place in a bowl or resealable plastic bag.

Combine the lemon juice, anchovies, garlic, parsley, oregano, mustard, and a large pinch of pepper in a food processor and puree until smooth. With the machine running, add the olive oil in a slow, steady stream.

Pour the marinade over the fish and turn gently to coat. Cover and refrigerate for 3 to 6 hours.

Beat the eggs in a wide, shallow bowl until well blended. Place the flour in a separate wide, shallow bowl and season generously with salt and pepper. Set a cooling rack over parchment paper or a baking sheet next to the bowls. Place a second cooling rack over parchment or a baking sheet and set nearby.

Working with one fillet at a time, dip a fillet in the flour to coat on both sides; shake off the excess. Dip in the egg, let the excess drip off, then place on the rack. (Tip: It helps to use a fork to lift the fillets in and out of the egg and flour.) Let the fillets rest for 5 minutes.

Dredge each fillet again in the flour. Shake off any excess and put on the clean rack. When all the fish have been dredged, wash and dry the first cooling rack and set in a baking pan near the stove to hold the fillets as they finish cooking.

Heat ¾ inch of oil in a large, deep skillet or Dutch oven over medium-high heat until it reaches 350°F. Adjust the heat, as needed, to maintain the temperature. Working in batches of three or four at a time, fry the fillets until golden brown on one side, about 2 minutes. Turn them over and cook on the other side until golden, about 2 minutes more. Transfer with a slotted spoon to the clean cooling rack to drain. Pat gently with paper towels. Sprinkle with salt while still warm.

continues

TO MAKE THE AGLIATA

Tear the bread, place in a small bowl, and sprinkle it with the Champagne vinegar and wine. Allow to soak, turning occasionally, until softened and the liquid is absorbed, about 15 minutes.

Transfer the bread to a food processor or blender along with the garlic, parsley, and a pinch of salt. Blend at low speed or pulse until the ingredients are finely ground. Add the egg yolks and blend just to incorporate (don't overblend or it will get too warm). With the machine running, add the neutral oil in a slow, steady stream to create an emulsion. Use a pusher to help incorporate or stop and scrape the sides as needed.

Transfer the mixture to a bowl and whisk in the olive oil by hand. You can thin the sauce with a little water if it seems too thick and firm or oily and on the verge of breaking. Don't let it break. As Brian says, you're the boss! Taste and adjust seasoning with salt and pepper. The sauce will keep, refrigerated, for about a week.

TO FINISH

Serve the fish hot with lemon wedges and the agliata.

Salmon in Agrodolce

SERVES 6

❮ ❮

Everyone needs a go-to salmon recipe, and when I was working at Genoa, this was definitely it. It delivers so much satisfaction with so little effort, and it's a super-easy way to serve a crowd. The simple lemon-mustard marinade has a fragrant touch of fennel, but it's the ample scoop of sugar that makes it so irresistible. The sugar caramelizes under the intense heat of the grill and plays with the lemon to create a mouthwatering agrodolce (sour-sweet) flavor profile. When you use luxuriously rich and fatty king salmon (aka chinook), it's even better.

1½ pound salmon fillet, skin removed	1½ teaspoons sea salt
3 tablespoons Dijon mustard	1 teaspoon fennel seeds, toasted and ground
3 tablespoons sugar	
2 tablespoons freshly squeezed lemon juice	Vegetable oil for grill grates
	1 tablespoon extra-virgin olive oil for drizzling
1½ tablespoons chopped fresh fennel fronds, plus 6 fronds for serving	6 lemon wedges for serving

Cut the salmon into six 4-ounce portions. Arrange in a 9-by-13-inch glass or ceramic baking dish.

Whisk together the mustard, sugar, lemon juice, chopped fennel fronds, salt, and ground fennel seeds in a small bowl until the sugar is dissolved.

Brush the marinade evenly and generously over the fish. Lay plastic wrap directly on the fish and set another baking dish on top to weigh down the fish. Refrigerate overnight.

Prepare a grill for direct cooking over medium-high heat (400° to 450°F). Scrub the grates clean and oil lightly. Add the salmon, drizzle each lightly with olive oil, and cook for 6 minutes. Use a fish spatula to carefully turn the fillets over, then grill 3 to 4 minutes more, or until the flesh flakes easily with a fork. (If you have a kitchen torch, feel free to brûlée the top if the grill wasn't hot enough to get the job done. Caramelization is an important part of the dish.)

Serve with a fennel frond on top and a lemon wedge on the side.

● ●

NOTE: *Alternatively, you can cook the fish in a convection oven set to 475°F. Cook on the middle rack (6 inches from the heat element) for 4 minutes. Turn and broil for 2 minutes more, or until the flesh flakes easily with a fork.*

The Cure for the Bare-Bones Beach House

At some point in the summer, you'll likely find yourself cooking in a summer kitchen that's not your own, some lovely rental place at the beach or on a lake with stellar views and a crapshoot kitchen. Sure, you might luck out with a well-stocked place sporting every tool you need, but more than likely it'll have nothing more than an odd collection of flimsy pans and a dull knife. Still, even the most underequipped kitchens can produce lovely meals if you keep things simple, as I've done with the recipes in this book. Assuming every vacation house kitchen has at least one large pot, a skillet, and a set of measuring cups and spoons, all you really need to bring along is a sharp knife, a whisk, spatula, a Microplane, and an instant-read thermometer, and you'll be able to make a majority of the recipes in this book. Of course, it doesn't hurt to bring a few other things, too. I always pack an apron and a vegetable peeler, and if I'm really nervous, I bring a large sauté pan and a saucepan, too. After once renting a really nice oceanfront beach house that only had one wineglass and one mason jar in the kitchen, I learned my lesson.

Halibut Baked with Aioli

SERVES 4

I first had this dish many years ago at a restaurant in Portland and was impressed by the way the aioli baked into a golden, pillowy soufflé while keeping the fish below succulent and luscious. I made it for a friend soon after, expecting to leave them similarly wowed, but instead she exclaimed, "Oh! Halibut Olympia! I haven't had that in years." Turns out, recipes for white fish baked under a blanket of mayonnaise have been around for over a century, with more variations than anyone can count. Most versions top the mayo with bread crumbs and cheese. Here, I keep things simple and let silky, garlic-scented aioli do all the heavy lifting. After all, fresh summer halibut is a beautiful thing best served by minimal fussing. It helps to whisk the aioli by hand for a softer texture than machine-made. It will cling to the fish like whipped cream, rather than slide off. If you don't want to spend the big bucks for halibut, black cod and lingcod are wonderful and far more affordable alternatives.

Extra-virgin olive oil

Four 4-ounce halibut fillets, or black cod
  or lingcod

Sea salt and freshly ground black pepper

1 batch Aioli (page 178)

¼ cup chopped fresh herbs, such as
  chives and basil

Preheat the oven to 500°F. Line a baking sheet with parchment paper and brush it with olive oil.

Season the fillets generously with salt and pepper. Place on the prepared baking sheet. Blend the herbs into the aioli and spread generously onto each fillet, about ⅓ cup per piece.

Place on the top rack of the oven. Cook until the fish is opaque and cooked through and the aioli is starting to color on top, 10 to 12 minutes.

Grilled Trout
WITH SALSA VERDE
SERVES 4

●●●●●●● ●●● ●● ●● ●●●●●●●● ●●● ●●● ●● ●●●●●●●● ●●● ●● ●● ●●●●●●

Fresh rainbow trout has so much going for it. It's economical, widely available, sustainably farmed, and very mild tasting, so it can accommodate almost any flavors you crave. It pairs especially well with bold herby sauces, such as Salsa Verde (page 169), when cooked on a charcoal grill until the skin gets crispy and kissed with smoke. Add grilled vegetables or roasted potatoes, a crisp salad, or tender green beans—whatever's in season at the market or in your garden.

Vegetable oil for grill grates

4 ounces pancetta, diced

4 fresh rainbow trout (about 1 pound each), butterflied, bones removed

Extra-virgin olive oil

Sea salt and freshly ground black pepper

2 lemons, 1 sliced thinly, 1 cut into quarters for serving

4 large fresh sage leaves

Salsa Verde (page 169) for serving

Prepare a charcoal grill for direct cooking over medium-high heat (400° to 450°F). Brush the cooking grates clean and lightly coat with vegetable oil.

On a stove, sauté the pancetta over medium-high heat until crisp, about 5 minutes. Remove with a slotted spoon and drain on paper towels.

Brush the inside and outside of the fish with olive oil and season generously inside and out with salt and pepper. Lay several thin slices of lemon and one sage leaf inside each fish. Sprinkle with pancetta bits. Fold the fish back up so the insides are facing.

Place the fish over direct heat on the grill. Cook for 4 minutes, or until grill marks appear. Use a fish spatula to carefully turn and cook them on the other side for 4 minutes more (if the fish doesn't release from the grill easily, it's not ready; give it another minute or two).

Remove from the heat and divide among warm plates. Spoon the salsa verde on top and serve with lemon wedges on the side.

The Wonderful World of Italian Peppers

From the top of the boot to the heel, sweet peppers thrive under the Italian sun, and specific regions are often known for producing certain varieties. But these days, all kinds of Italian peppers can be found side by side at farmers' markets in the States. Look for chubby little cherry peppers akin to the Sicilian peperoncino tondo Calabrese, or corno di toro, which has a long, curved shape like a bull's horn. Even more common are Jimmy Nardellos, skinny, twisting, wrinkled peppers brought to the States from the Basilicata region in the late 1880s. Italian peppers tend to be longer and skinnier, with thinner skin than traditional bell peppers. If using them, you may want to double the quantity and skip the peeling step.

Chicken with Tomatoes and Red Peppers
(POLLO ALLA ROMANA)
SERVES 4

((((((((((((((

This braised chicken dish is as Roman as it gets. Every trattoria and osteria (pub) in the ancient city has a version on its lunch menu, and every summer, it makes several appearances on my own table, too—usually within days (or even hours) of spying the arrival of red bell peppers at the farmers' market. This is one of those dishes that tastes even better when allowed to cool to lukewarm, making it ideal for a picnic.

Many recipes for Pollo Alla Romana call for some kind of cured pork product in the form of prosciutto, pancetta, or guanciale. But as much as I love porky flavor, I tend to leave it out, so the flavor of the chicken can take the spotlight. Of course, that's only worth it if the chicken is a flavorful pasture-raised bird that spent its days running around and eating bugs and seeds. If using a run-of-the-mill chicken, two ounces of chopped cured pork, sautéed along with the chicken, will add some welcome complexity. Leaving chicken hindquarters whole makes for a more elegant presentation, but separating thighs and legs will add more juices to the sauce. You can completely change the flavor by substituting roasted green bell peppers for the red bell peppers, or by combining yellow and red bell peppers. Either way, it's a lovely dish.

4 bone-in, skin-on chicken hindquarters, or 4 drumsticks and 4 thighs, or 8 thighs
Sea salt and freshly ground black pepper
5 tablespoons extra-virgin olive oil
4 garlic cloves, slightly smashed
2 ounces pancetta, chopped (optional)

½ cup dry white wine, preferably Frascati
1½ cups tomato puree
1 tablespoon chopped fresh marjoram, or 1 teaspoon dried crushed
3 red bell peppers, roasted (see Roasted Peppers in Crema, page 105) or grilled (see Peperonata, page 48), peeled, and cut into 2-inch strips

Season the chicken all over with salt. Arrange in a single layer on a plate and refrigerate, uncovered, overnight. (This technique, called dry-brining, will ensure moist, flavorful meat.)

Preheat the oven to 350°F. Pat the chicken dry and season with black pepper.

continues

Heat the oil in a 12-inch sauté pan with a lid or a Dutch oven over medium-high heat. Working in batches if necessary, fry the chicken, skin side down, until golden, about 10 minutes. Turn the chicken over, add the garlic, and brown the chicken on the other side, turning the garlic as needed to lightly brown and keep it from burning. Remove the chicken and garlic and repeat with any remaining chicken. If using pancetta, add it to the pan and gently cook until the fat renders and the meat is crispy. Remove with a slotted spoon and set aside.

Return all the chicken, skin side up, to the pan along with the garlic. Add the white wine. Cook over low heat until two-thirds of the wine has evaporated, about 5 minutes.

Add the tomato puree and marjoram. The liquid should come about three-quarters up the side of the chicken. If necessary, add a little water. Season with salt. Bring the mixture to a simmer over medium heat and place in the oven. Bake for 1 hour, or until the meat is tender, checking occasionally and adding water, ¼ cup at a time, if it looks as if the mixture is drying out too much.

When the chicken is tender, add the roasted bell peppers and the cooked pancetta (if using). Cook for another 10 minutes, stirring a few times. Season with salt to taste.

Serve the chicken hot or at room temperature along with crusty bread or polenta. If the skin did not crisp and you prefer crispy skin, transfer the chicken pieces to a baking sheet and heat under the broiler for a few minutes until crisp, watching carefully to make sure it doesn't burn.

Grilled Vinegar-Marinated Chicken
(POLLO ALLA DIAVOLA)
SERVES 4

A marinade of zingy oregano-infused vinegar and a generous rub of fresh herbs make for the most succulent grilled chicken, while the spicy kick from red pepper flakes and the hint of char from the grill inspire this dish's devilish name. Any leftovers are superb sliced and tucked into a sandwich or tossed into salad for lunch. This recipe, from my talented Umbrian chef friend Salvatore Denaro, requires a little advance planning. The chicken should marinate for at least an hour or two, and you'll need to make the infused vinegar at least two days ahead. Be sure to use dried oregano that hasn't been lingering at the back of your cupboard for eons. The woodsy perfume of Sicilian oregano, in particular, really pairs well with the smoke from the grill. If you don't like spice, just skip the red pepper flakes. It'll still be fabulous.

½ cup red wine vinegar

1 tablespoon dried Sicilian oregano

½ cup extra-virgin olive oil

One 3- to 3½-pound chicken, spatch-cocked, wing tips removed (see Note)

3 tablespoons chopped fresh sage

1 tablespoon finely chopped fresh rosemary leaves

1 tablespoon coarsely ground black pepper

2 teaspoons sea salt

1 teaspoon red pepper flakes (optional)

Grapeseed oil or other high-smoke point oil for grill grates

Combine the vinegar with the dried oregano in a small glass jar. Let steep at room temperature for at least 2 days and up to 2 weeks. When ready to use, stir in the olive oil.

Set the spatchcocked chicken, skin side down, in an enameled or glass baking pan to catch the liquid. Drizzle the vinegar mixture over the chicken and rub it in. Allow to marinate for 1 to 2 hours at room temperature or up to 6 hours in the refrigerator (if refrigerated, let sit out at room temperature for 1 hour before cooking).

Mix together the sage, rosemary, black pepper, salt, and red pepper flakes in a small bowl. Rub the mixture together with your fingers to lightly crush the herbs and release their oils.

continues

Remove the chicken from the pan and reserve the marinade for basting. Pat the chicken dry. Rub the herbs all over both sides of the chicken.

Prepare a grill (preferably charcoal or wood) for indirect cooking over medium heat (350° to 400°F). Scrub the grates clean and lightly oil with grapeseed oil.

Place the chicken, skin side down, on the cool side of the grill and cook with the lid on and the top vent half open until the skin releases easily from the grates, 15 to 20 minutes. Turn the chicken over and baste with the reserved marinade. Continue to cook with the cover on for 30 to 45 minutes more, basting with the marinade every 15 to 20 minutes, until a thermometer inserted in the thickest part of the breast registers 140°F and the thighs register 155°F.

Transfer the chicken to a cutting board and tent with foil. Allow to rest for at least 15 minutes before carving to allow the meat time to reabsorb the juices (discard any remaining marinade). Cut the hindquarters from the chicken and separate the legs and thighs. Cut the two breast halves off the bone and cut each in half. Arrange the chicken on a platter, pour any accumulated juices over the top, and serve.

❮ ❮

NOTE: *To spatchcock a chicken, place it, breast side down, on a cutting board and use poultry shears to cut along each side of the backbone to remove it. Turn the chicken over and press firmly on the breastbone with the heel of your hand until it cracks and allows the bird to slightly flatten. Tuck the wing tips behind the breast or remove completely to keep them from charring.*

Bistecca alla Fiorentina, Nostrana Style

SERVES 2, OR 4 WITH AMPLE SIDE DISHES

• •

In Tuscany, bistecca usually comes from Chianina cattle, an ancient Tuscan breed, and it's cooked precisely but simply to let the beefy flavor take center stage. You won't find that breed in the States, but you should still choose the best-quality beef you can find. We prefer a 2-inch-thick steak at the restaurant and cook it indirectly over a wood fire to a beautiful medium-rare, turning regularly to encourage a robust, savory crust with very little bitter char. To serve, we slice the steak thinly and bathe it in olive oil infused with garlic and rosemary. It's such a simple dish, but when done right, it's otherworldly. This is the time to bring out your best Chianti Riserva or a Brunello di Montalcino.

⅓ cup extra-virgin olive oil

7 garlic cloves, sliced paper-thin

Leaves from 2 rosemary sprigs, chopped finely

One 2.2-pound (1 kg), 2-inch-thick, bone-in rib eye

Salt

Grapeseed oil or other high-smoke-point oil for grill grates

Freshly ground black pepper

1 lemon, cut into wedges

Prepare a charcoal grill for indirect cooking over medium-high heat (400° to 450°F; see Note).

Heat the olive oil, garlic, and rosemary in a small saucepan over medium-low heat on the stovetop. Very slowly simmer until the garlic and rosemary are completely softened, taking care not to let the garlic get any color, 25 to 30 minutes. Keep warm.

Meanwhile, remove the steak from the refrigerator 15 minutes before cooking. Pat the steak dry and sprinkle salt over all sides (including the edges) until it is completely coated in a fine shower of salt. (The pepper will burn, so add it after cooking.)

Scrub the grates clean and lightly oil with grapeseed oil. Place the steak on the grill over indirect heat and cook, undisturbed, for 7 minutes. Turn the steak over and repeat on the other side. Flip the steak back to the first side, turning a quarter turn, and cook for 7 more

continues

minutes. Repeat on the other side. Watch for flare-ups from the dripping fat, and move the steak away from the flames as necessary to keep the flames from charring it.

After cooking both sides twice, the steak should be developing a dark brown crust with only a tiny bit of char. Keep cooking a few minutes more, turning it and moving it away from flare-ups as necessary, until a meat thermometer inserted horizontally into the center of the steak reaches 125°F, then remove from the heat and transfer to a cutting board.

Trim the bone away from the steak (no need to let the meat rest yet). Place the bone, cut side down, on the grill and sear for 30 seconds. Return the steak, cut side down, to the grill, leaning it against the bone for support. Sear for about 30 seconds. Transfer both back to the cutting board. Shower the steak generously with ground pepper on both sides. Allow to rest for 14 minutes. Keep the grill hot.

When the steak has rested, briefly return it to the grill to rewarm the surface, about 10 seconds per side. Cut into ½-inch-thick slices across the grain, perpendicular to where the bone was attached, following its gently arched shape.

To serve, set the bone on the plate and fan out the slices alongside. Spoon the garlic-rosemary oil over the slices and serve with lemon wedges on the side.

* *

NOTE: *This steak is sublime when cooked over a wood fire, as we do at the restaurant. Build a wood fire as you would a campfire, and when the wood starts to turn ashy and gray, restrict the airflow so that the flames die down. When the logs become red-hot coals, they're ready. Bank them to one side, place the grate 6 inches above, and cook the steak over the side opposite the coals.*

For the Love of Beefsteak

The first time I ever set foot in Italy, it was on a trip to Florence in my early 30s. We had taken an overnight train from Paris, arrived early in the morning, and in my first memory I'm standing groggily in a caffè in the Piazza San Marco, trying to figure out how to pay, as the streets filled with art students zipping off to class on their Vespas. I just remember feeling completely overwhelmed by the noise and the energy and beauty of it all—especially as I watched this young, gorgeous Adonis standing next to me devour a whipped cream–filled *cornetto* with gusto. I thought I would melt! Everything in Italy just felt so much more sensory, more sensual—just so much *more*. I was in love and still am. It was on this trip that I first visited Trattoria Mario, a popular hole-in-the-wall next to the pig statue at the main central market. We ordered Tuscany's famed bistecca, and the waiter brought out a giant hunk of raw meat. After a little confusion, we realized he wanted us to decide how big we wanted it. I'll never forget that first trip and that first bistecca, over-the-top thick and grilled until rare with a deeply savory burnished crust. It's one of my favorite dishes at Nostrana and well worth building a feast around in the summer.

Turchetta

SERVES 4, WITH LEFTOVERS

The heat of summer often calls for lighter forms of protein, such as chicken or turkey breast, but let's face it, turkey is pretty boring—unless you give it the porchetta treatment. Tuscan porchetta is generally a boneless pork loin or pork shoulder that's butterflied and spread with garlic, rosemary, sage, and fennel seeds, rolled up, wrapped in pork belly with its skin, and roasted. In this recipe, from my food writer friend Judy Witts Francini, a butterflied turkey breast stands in for the pork roast. I skip the overwhelming decadence of the pork belly, layering slices of savory prosciutto and showers of Parmesan inside the breast instead. Once it's sliced, you end up with these meaty pinwheels of deliciousness, with a crispy exterior and a savory, moist interior—and the leftovers are ideal for sandwiches and picnics.

One 2- to 3-pound boneless half turkey breast, skin on

Sea salt and freshly ground black pepper

9 garlic cloves, 8 very thinly sliced, 1 unpeeled and smashed lightly

Leaves only from 1 large bunch sage (20 to 30 small to medium leaves)

1 cup finely grated Parmigiano-Reggiano

4 teaspoons fennel seeds, toasted and ground

6 ounces thinly sliced prosciutto

5 tablespoons extra-virgin olive oil

1 rosemary sprig

1 cup white wine or rosé

1 cup chicken broth

1 tablespoon unsalted butter

Lay the turkey breast, skin side down, on a cutting board. Use a sharp knife to make a vertical cut down the middle, only going about two-thirds of the way through. You do not want to cut it in half completely or cut to the skin.

Holding the blade parallel to the surface of the meat, butterfly one side of the breast by making a horizontal cut about halfway through the thickness of the meat, starting at the bottom of the breast and stopping when the meat is still attached by about ¾ inch at the other edge. Repeat on the other breast, using the cut from the first side as a guide. The turkey breast should now be able to open up flat like an open book. Use the smooth side of a meat mallet to pound it out gently so the thickness is uniform and you have a nice rectangular shape.

Season the turkey with salt and pepper. Distribute the garlic slices and sage leaves evenly over the surface of the meat. Mix the Parmesan and fennel together, then sprinkle evenly on top. Layer the prosciutto slices on top of that. Roll up the breast from one narrow end to the other, leaving the skin exposed. Tie with kitchen twine to form a compact roll. Season the outside with salt and pepper.

Preheat the oven to 400°F.

Heat the olive oil, along with the mashed garlic clove and rosemary sprig, in a roasting pan over medium heat on the stovetop. Add the rolled turkey and brown on all sides, about 8 minutes per side. Pour in the wine and chicken broth, bring to a simmer, and transfer the pan to the oven. Roast until the internal temperature reaches 145°F, 25 to 30 minutes. Transfer the turkey to a cutting board and let rest for 15 to 20 minutes. If the pan juices are not already a saucelike consistency, set the roasting pan over medium heat and simmer until slightly reduced. Remove from the heat and whisk in the butter.

Carve the turkey crosswise into thick slices to reveal a pinwheel pattern. Serve with the sauce. Use leftovers for sandwiches or a charcuterie board.

Pork with Tuna Sauce
(MAIALE TONNATO)

SERVES 6

❛❛❛

Far more elegant than a platter of cold cuts, this twist on the Piedmontese classic is perfect for those steamy summer nights when you crave something hearty but not hot. It's also a perfect picnic entrée. Although traditionally made with veal, this version uses a more economical (and, in my mind, more flavorful) pork loin roast instead. The thinly sliced meat is served chilled and layered with a creamy sauce that's akin to a fishy mayonnaise, transforming the mild pork into something luscious and intriguing. Feel free to be lavish with the sauce (in Italy, sometimes this dish is more sauce than meat!), but if you have any left over, it makes a wonderful dip for vegetables.

PORK ROAST

3 garlic cloves

2½ teaspoons sea salt

2½ to 3 pounds boneless pork loin roast

1½ teaspoons freshly ground black pepper

1 tablespoon extra-virgin olive oil

½ cup white wine

TUNA SAUCE

One 3- to 4-ounce can imported, oil-packed tuna

5 anchovy fillets

3 tablespoons capers, rinsed (if packed in salt, soak in water for 10 minutes and drain)

2 garlic cloves

3 tablespoons freshly squeezed lemon juice

½ cup extra-virgin olive oil

½ to 1 cup mayonnaise (see Aioli, page 178), or use Duke's brand

GARNISH

Thin lemon slices

Whole fresh parsley leaves

Black Taggiasca olives, or any other flavorful black olive, pitted and cut into halves or fourths

Whole capers

Anchovy fillets, torn

TO MAKE THE PORK ROAST

Pound the garlic and salt together in a mortar and pestle to form a soft paste. Pat the pork dry. Rub the paste all over the pork. Season with pepper. Let sit for 30 minutes.

Preheat the oven to 350°F. Heat the olive oil in a small roasting pan over medium-high heat. Add the pork and cook until browned on all sides, about 5 minutes per side. Transfer

the pan to the oven and roast for 25 minutes. Add the wine, baste the meat with the liquid, and continue to roast until the meat feels firm when pressed and the internal temperature reaches 135°F, 25 to 35 more minutes.

Transfer the meat to a cutting board, tent with foil, and allow to rest until completely cool. Refrigerate if not using right away.

TO MAKE THE TUNA SAUCE

Drain the tuna and place it in a food processor along with the anchovies, capers, garlic, lemon juice, and olive oil. Process until creamy and well blended. Transfer to a small bowl and gently fold in the mayonnaise to taste. Taste for seasoning.

TO ASSEMBLE

Use a very sharp knife to slice the pork into thin slices, as close to ⅛ inch thick as possible.

Smear the bottom of a serving platter with some of the tuna sauce. Arrange a single layer of pork slices on top, meeting edge to edge without overlapping. Cover the pork with more sauce, then make another layer. Repeat the layers until all the pork is used, leaving enough sauce to completely coat the topmost layer.

Arrange the garnishes over the meat before serving. Cover leftovers with plastic wrap and chill well. It will keep for at least a week.

Pork Tenderloin in Baguette
(FILETTO DI MAIALE IN CROSTA)
SERVES 4 TO 6

I had my first taste of this roasted, large-format sandwich in the Tuscan hilltop town of San Miniato, courtesy of a fourth-generation butcher named Andrea Falaschi. It's a recipe with roots—the original came from his grandmother, who passed it on to his mother, and his mother passed it on to him. But I have to admit, once it landed in my hands, I kind of messed it up. I forgot that Andrea wraps the whole tenderloin-stuffed baguette in pancetta, which helps hold it all together. I put the pancetta over the pork to baste the meat as it cooks. I'm pretty pleased with my version, actually, but both versions will roast into savory, sliceable heaven. Crispy outside, juicy inside, it's both simple and impressive, like a porky riff on beef Wellington without all the fuss. It's also great for dinner parties and to take along on picnics. It's fantastic served with pepper jelly or Dijon mustard. Just be sure to choose a tenderloin that's not massive because you don't want it to overwhelm the bread. Cut it in half lengthwise, if you must, and save the rest for another use. And cut the bread to fit the length of the meat.

1 to 1½ pounds pork tenderloin

Sea salt and freshly ground black pepper

⅓ cup minced fennel fronds or fresh flat-leaf parsley, or a mixture of both

1 tablespoon minced fresh sage

1 tablespoon minced fresh rosemary

3 garlic cloves, minced

2 teaspoons fennel pollen

2 tablespoons red wine

2 tablespoons extra-virgin olive oil

1 baguette

Two ¼-inch-thick slices pancetta

Pepper jelly, Dijon mustard, Salmoriglio (page 170), or Salsa Verde (page 169) for serving

Preheat the oven to 350°F. Trim any extra fat or gristle from the tenderloin and season it with salt and black pepper.

Mix together the fennel fronds, sage, rosemary, garlic, fennel pollen, wine, and olive oil in a small bowl. Season with salt and black pepper.

Cut the baguette to the size of the tenderloin (about 10 inches).

Split it lengthwise so it opens like a book. Scrape away some of the bread on each side so the tenderloin can nestle inside.

Spread the herb paste inside the baguette. Place the tenderloin inside and cover with the pancetta slices, layering them like shingles. Close up the bread around the tenderloin and tie with kitchen twine every 2 inches to hold the opening tightly closed.

Wrap the baguette in foil, place on a baking sheet, and roast for 25 minutes. Remove the foil and continue to roast for another 20 minutes, or until a thermometer inserted in the center of the meat reaches 140°F.

Remove the baguette from the oven and let it rest, loosely covered with foil, for 10 minutes. Cut off the twine, slice the baguette into thin slices or quarters, and serve with pepper jelly, mustard, salmoriglio, or salsa verde on the side.

Braised Pork Sausages
WITH GRAPES AND TOMATILLOS
SERVES 4

• •

This utterly simple, country-style dish always makes an appearance on vineyard tables (not to mention my own) in late summer, when the wine grapes are ready for harvest. In Italy, after a hard day's work among the vines, they'll just toss a few handfuls of wine grapes, seeds and all, right into a skillet of sausages and end up with a gorgeous medley of savory and sweet, perfect over polenta or alongside crusty bread. Add some sliced cheese and a bottle of wine, and revel in the delicious simplicity. Making your own sausages takes this dish to another level, but you can certainly use good-quality store-bought sausages instead and skip right to the assembly step.

SWEET ITALIAN PORK SAUSAGES

2 pounds boneless pork shoulder with fat cap, well chilled

8 ounces pork fat, well chilled

1 tablespoon fennel seeds

1 tablespoon salt

1 tablespoon dried basil

1 tablespoon dried Sicilian oregano

1 tablespoon red pepper flakes (for spicy sausages; optional)

1 teaspoon black peppercorns

3 garlic cloves

⅓ cup white or red wine

4 to 6 feet of natural hog casings, cleaned (optional)

ASSEMBLY

2 tablespoons extra-virgin olive oil

4 large or 8 small sweet Italian pork sausages (homemade or store-bought)

10 ounces seedless black or red grapes, stems removed

6 tomatillos, quartered

Flaky sea salt

Pinch of fennel pollen (optional)

Polenta or Bruschetta (page 6) for serving

TO MAKE THE SAUSAGES

Cut the pork shoulder and pork fat into chunks small enough (1 to 2 inches) to fit through the feeder of a meat grinder. Freeze for 30 to 60 minutes, until cold and firm. Fit the grinder with the coarse blade and feed the chunks into the grinder, alternating between the pork and the fat. Knead the mixture together to blend well, then spread out on a baking sheet into a 1-inch-thick rectangle.

Place the fennel seeds in a small, dry skillet and set over medium heat. Toast until fragrant and just starting to brown. Transfer to a small bowl and add the salt, basil, oregano, and red pepper flakes (if using). Add the peppercorns to the pan and return it to medium heat; toast until fragrant, 3 to 5 minutes. Transfer to a mortar and pestle and coarsely crush, then add the garlic to the peppercorns and crush into a paste. Stir the peppercorn mixture into the bowl of spices.

Sprinkle the spice mixture over the pork. Knead together and spread out again in the pan. Press your fingers into the surface to make dimples all over. Fill the dimples with wine, then knead everything together. Chill for 1 hour before stuffing into the hog casings (if using).

While the mixture chills, soak the casings in cold water for at least 30 minutes. Use a sausage stuffer to stuff the mixture into the casings according to the manufacturer's instructions, then pinch into 4- to 5-inch sausages. Alternatively, forgo the casings and shape the pork mixture into 3-inch-diameter patties.

Sausages in casings should be air-dried on a rack for 1 to 2 hours, then refrigerated on a paper towel–lined plate, uncovered, overnight, to dry out the casings before using or freezing. If making patties, refrigerate or freeze them if not using right away. (Makes 2½ pounds of sausage.)

TO ASSEMBLE

Heat the oil in a 12-inch sauté pan over medium heat. Add the sausages and brown well on all sides, about 3 minutes per side. Add the grapes and tomatillos. Lower the heat to medium-low and cook until the grapes are heated through and begin to burst, 10 to 15 minutes, turning the sausages often, and adding a splash of water or white wine if the grapes and tomatillos don't seem juicy enough. Season with salt to taste and fennel pollen, if using.

To serve, spoon the grapes and sausages over a platter or individual bowls of polenta, or serve as is with bruschetta on the side.

Sausage from Scratch

Making your own sausages is a project, for sure, but a worthy one, particularly on lazy summer days when there's not much else to do but putter happily in the kitchen. It takes a fair amount of time, but it's not technically difficult, and the results are incredible—not only because of the high satisfaction quotient but because you can customize the flavorings and avoid the corn syrup and sugar so common in commercial sausages. Just cook little meatballs of the mixture as you go to test the flavors until you get it just right. The wonderfully simple and savory recipe in this book comes by way of Zeph Shepard, owner and head butcher at Proletariat Sausage in Portland, where I took a sausage-making class and fell in love with the process.

To go the whole nine yards, you'll need hog casings (you can usually buy these from a butcher that makes their own sausages), plus a meat grinder and a sausage stuffer, both of which are sold as stand-alone devices or as attachments for stand mixers. However, you can also use preground pork and mince the pork fat yourself. And you can forgo stuffing the sausage into links and hand form the mixture into patties instead.

It's surprising how easy and satisfying making sausages can be. Just be sure to keep the meat and fat ice-cold—not frozen, but nearly so. Just pop it in the freezer for 30 minutes to an hour before you start grinding. You should freeze your bowls and grinder, too. This will ensure the meat and fat mix together cleanly without becoming greasy muck.

Thin Parmesan-Crusted Lamb Chops

SERVES 4

Once or twice a summer, you'll inevitably crave something fried. I call it the carnival effect. You get a whiff of fryer oil on a warm summer night, and suddenly you're craving funnel cakes and corn dogs. These chops, of course, are a far more grown-up way to satisfy the craving. Inspired by a recipe from Marcella Hazan, they're pressed until thin and given a generous shower of Parmesan in the breading. Think of them as lamb lollipops, perfect for nibbling with one hand while you sip a cocktail from the other. Although three chops per person is a generous portion, they're so delicious you may want to level up to four.

Two 8-rib lamb rib racks, frenched and cut into chops (or at least 12 single-rib frenched lamb chops; see Note)

Sea salt and freshly ground black pepper

1½ cups (180 g) all-purpose flour

3 large eggs

1 cup finely grated Parmigiano-Reggiano (preferably aged 1½ to 2 years)

1 cup fine, dry, unflavored bread crumbs

Extra-virgin olive oil for frying

Lemon wedges for garnish

If cooking the chops in batches, preheat the oven to 200° to 250°F. Line a baking sheet with parchment paper.

Fill a small bowl with cold water. Dip a meat pounder in the water and use it to push, rather than pound, the meaty part of each chop until it is about ⅓ inch thick—it should be an even thickness and the size of a very small saucer. If the meat contracts, try letting it rest and pushing it again. Season both sides with salt and pepper.

In a shallow dish, combine the flour with ½ teaspoon of salt and ½ teaspoon of pepper. Beat the eggs in a separate wide dish. Mix the Parmesan and bread crumbs in a pie plate or separate shallow dish.

Working with one chop at a time, dip each side in the seasoned flour to coat. Shake off the excess. Dip into the beaten egg, letting the excess egg drip back into the bowl. Press both sides into the bread crumb mixture. Place on the prepared baking sheet. Repeat with the remaining chops.

Pour ½ inch of olive oil into a large skillet and heat over medium heat until hot but not smoking. Add enough chops to fill the skillet without overcrowding (you may need two skillets, or cook them in batches). Cook until golden on one side, 3 to 5 minutes. Turn and cook the other side until golden. If cooking in batches, transfer to a baking sheet fitted with a cooling rack and place in the warm oven while you cook the remaining chops.

Serve hot with lemon wedges.

● ●

NOTE: *"Frenched" means to remove all the excess meat, fat, and membrane from the bone of a chop to give it a clean appearance. It also makes it less messy to hold these "lollipop" chops by the bone when eating. Ask your butcher to french the lamb rack for you. To do it yourself, set the rack meaty side down. Slice away any meat and fat on top of the ribs until only a thin layer of fat remains on top of the meat. Turn the rack over and slice the membrane open along the center of each bone. Use a clean towel to grip the flesh at the end of the bones and hold it down while lifting the ribs up until 2 to 3 inches of bone have lifted up and out from the membrane. Turn the rack over and cut away the flap of meat. Use your knife to scrape away any lingering bits of meat or membrane on the exposed bones. Cut between each bone to create individual chops. You might have quite a bit of meat scraps left over. Freeze them to add to a meat ragù or sauté with onions and tuck into a roll for a tasty snack.*

DESSERTS

Yogurt Panna Cotta

SERVES 4

● ●

Panna cotta is a lovely make-ahead dessert any time of year, but it's particularly welcome in the summer, when it offers a silky-cool, light, and creamy backdrop to all the luscious fruits in season—especially fresh berries, cherries, or other stone fruits. If you want to get a little fancy, poached fruit, compote, or Piedmontese Baked Peaches (page 158) are fabulous accompaniments. Stirring in a cup of plain yogurt adds a tangy richness that makes it even more irresistible, sort of a hint of cheesecake but without the heft. Keep in mind the dairy is the star of the show here, so choose wisely. I love Nancy's brand yogurt because it's Oregon made and wonderfully tart, but the complex richness of sheep's milk yogurt is another great option, or a whole milk yogurt from a local creamery.

1½ tablespoons water

1½ teaspoons unflavored powdered gelatin

1 cup heavy cream

½ cup sugar

1 cup plain whole-milk yogurt

Pinch of salt

Fresh fruit, poached fruit, or compote for serving

Pour the water in a small bowl and sprinkle the gelatin over the top. Let stand for 3 minutes, without stirring, to soften the gelatin.

Warm the cream and sugar in a heavy saucepan over medium-low heat, stirring occasionally, until steaming. Remove from the heat and whisk in the gelatin until fully dissolved. Allow to cool for a few minutes, then gradually whisk in the yogurt and salt.

Divide the mixture among four ½-cup ramekins and refrigerate until cold and set, at least 3 hours or overnight.

To serve, run a knife around the edge of the ramekins and unmold onto plates (or serve in the ramekins). Top with fresh fruit, poached fruit, or seasonal compote. These are also delicious with Almond Cream (page 159) in addition to the fruit, or instead of it, poured over the top.

Lemon and Rosemary Granita

SERVES 8

In Italy, a dinner of fish pasta or whole fish isn't complete without lemon granita for dessert. It's a light and refreshing end to a meal and can even serve as a palate cleanser between courses. This version, from Nostrana pastry chef Maddie Stratton, is as easy to make as lemonade. You just need time to let it freeze so you can scrape it with a fork into a snowlike slush. One of my favorite ways to serve granita is in a cocktail called sgroppino. Just scoop it into a glass and top with Prosecco, although any sparkling wine will work, or even soda water if you want something zero-proof. This version adds rosemary for the barest hint of herbal complexity that elevates the lemon flavor.

ROSEMARY SYRUP
1 cup sugar

½ cup cold filtered water

2 large rosemary sprigs

LEMON GRANITA
1 cup rosemary syrup

1½ cups cold filtered water

Zest of 4 lemons

1½ cups freshly squeezed lemon juice (from about 6 lemons)

¼ cup limoncello (optional)

Fine sea salt

TO MAKE THE ROSEMARY SYRUP

Bring the sugar and water to a boil in a medium pot over high heat, stirring to dissolve the sugar. Remove from the heat and add the rosemary sprigs. Allow to cool, then transfer to an airtight container and refrigerate. You should have 1 cup. Allow the rosemary to infuse for 24 hours before removing.

TO MAKE THE LEMON GRANITA

Mix together the rosemary syrup, water, lemon zest, lemon juice, and limoncello (if using) in a medium bowl. Season to taste with salt. Transfer to a baking dish (the bigger the dish, the faster the granita will freeze). At this point, you have two options: freeze for several hours or overnight until hard, then scrape the granita with a fork to create a snowy or slushy consistency; or freeze for several hours, stirring the mixture every 30 minutes, or until it reaches a slushy consistency.

Scoop into glasses and serve.

Almond Granita

SERVES 8

¢ ¢

Granita was born in Sicily, and its roots reach back centuries to the days when the snow from Mount Etna was a key ingredient. Almond is one of the most classic flavors, and the nuts give the granita a creamier texture than fruit versions. With such a long history comes a long tradition; in this case, serving almond granita topped with whipped cream, and a brioche bun on the side. Of course, you can skip those additions if you want to keep things light, or serve it with a shot of espresso poured over it and a dollop of whipped cream if you need a pick-me-up. Even the almond cream for the base is incredibly versatile. Try using it to make the traditional iced coffee drink of Lecce: iced espresso with a spoonful of the almond cream to sweeten and enrich it. Using a jar of Caffè Sicilia Noto Romana almond spread, made with real Sicilian almonds, will give you the most authentic flavor with the least amount of effort, but it comes at a very precious price point. In this version, Nostrana pastry chef Maddie Stratton reverse-engineers the spread, making a deeply flavorful almond cream for the base. This recipe yields more almond cream than you'll need for one batch of granita, but the generous quantity is easier to puree and it'll keep refrigerated for several months. Using imported Sicilian almonds will give you the most intense and traditional almond flavor. But regular almonds with a hefty splash of extract work great, too.

ITALIAN ALMOND CREAM (MAKES 4 CUPS)

2 cups sugar

2 cups plus 5 ounces cold filtered water

14 ounces blanched almonds (preferably Sicilian almonds)

2 tablespoons almond extract (if not using Sicilian almonds)

Sea salt

ALMOND GRANITA

8 ounces Italian almond cream

2½ cups cold filtered water

TO MAKE THE ITALIAN ALMOND CREAM

Bring the sugar and 2 cups of the water to a boil in a medium pot over high heat, stirring to dissolve the sugar. Continue to simmer until the mixture reaches 230°F. Remove from the heat and add the almonds. Allow to steep for 10 minutes.

Transfer the mixture to a food processor or blender and puree to a relatively smooth paste. Add the remaining 5 ounces of water and almond extract (if using) and pulse to combine. Season with salt to taste. If not using right away, transfer to an airtight container and refrigerate. The Italian almond cream will keep, refrigerated, for several months due to its high sugar content.

TO MAKE THE ALMOND GRANITA

Mix or blend the almond cream and water in a medium bowl until combined. Pass the mixture through a cheesecloth-lined sieve into a baking dish (the bigger the dish, the faster the granita will freeze). Discard the solids (or put in a smoothie!). At this point, you have two options: freeze for several hours or overnight until hard, then scrape the granita with a fork to create a snowy or slushy consistency; or freeze for several hours, stirring the mix every 30 minutes, until it reaches a slushy consistency.

Scoop into glasses and serve.

Torrone Semifreddo

SERVES 6

I love semifreddo because it's so easy to throw together and can be flavored in countless ways. This version, adapted from *The Silver Spoon* cookbook, uses chewy, nutty, store-bought torrone (nut and honey nougat) to provide flavor and texture to the base mixture of whipped egg yolks lightened with whipped egg whites and whipped cream. But feel free to replace all or some of the nougat with fresh berries, peaches, or other stone fruit instead. Or increase the sugar by a few tablespoons and add an equal amount of unsweetened cocoa powder. Be sure to remove the dessert from the freezer 20 to 30 minutes before slicing and serving so the rock-hard mixture can soften into the perfect ice-creamy texture.

3 large eggs, separated

⅛ teaspoon cream of tartar

¼ cup superfine sugar

11 ounces torrone, chopped finely (see Note)

2 tablespoons brandy

1½ cups heavy cream, well chilled

Line a 9-inch loaf pan with plastic wrap so that it hangs over the edges on all four sides.

Whip the egg whites and cream of tartar on high speed in the bowl of a mixer until stiff peaks form, 3 to 5 minutes (the egg whites should stand straight up in a peak when you lift the whisk). Transfer to a large bowl.

Wash and dry the mixing bowl and add the egg yolks and sugar. If using a stand mixer, fit the mixer with the paddle attachment, or use your hand mixer and beat on high speed until pale and fluffy, about 5 minutes, stopping occasionally to scrape down the sides of

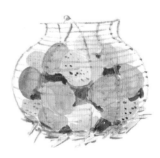

the bowl. Stir in the torrone and brandy. Gently fold the egg whites into the egg yolk mixture, then transfer back to the large bowl.

Wash the mixing bowl and rinse with cold water to chill it down. If using a stand mixer, fit it with the whisk attachment, or continue to use your hand mixer. Add the cream and whip until stiff peaks form (when you lift the whisk, the cream should stand straight up in a peak with just the tip barely flopping over). Gently fold the cream into the torrone mixture until well combined.

Pour the mixture into the prepared pan and cover with more plastic wrap to seal well. Freeze for at least 8 hours, or ideally overnight. Remove the semifreddo from the freezer 20 to 30 minutes before serving. Lift it out of the pan with the plastic wrap, then peel it off. Cut the semifreddo into 1½-inch-thick slices. Serve immediately while still cold and partially frozen.

● ●

NOTE: *Imported Italian torrone can either be hard (torrone friabile) or sticky (torrone tenero), but either way it can be tricky to cut, especially since it's so dense with whole nuts. To cut hard torrone, position the edge of a cleaver or heavy knife on it and gently tap the back of the knife with a mallet to chisel off pieces. For soft torrone, try oiling the blade of the knife to keep it from sticking. Press down firmly to cut through, rather than sawing back and forth.*

Cherry Semifreddo

MAKES 2 LOAVES; EACH SERVES 8

● ●

Semifreddo, Italian for "half-frozen," delivers all the joy of gelato but requires no special equipment, no prechilled canister—in fact, almost no preplanning except for the fact that it must chill until firm. This recipe is a simple and elegant way to showcase plump summertime cherries, and it makes two loaves: one for now, one for later. Believe me, you'll be grateful you made more than one. This is a perfect make-ahead recipe that can be stored for up to a week and brought out to impress guests at your next dinner party. A drizzle of aged balsamic adds visual drama and contributes a zesty element of surprise to the sweet and creamy elements of the dish.

6 large egg yolks	3 cups heavy cream, well chilled
1¼ cups superfine sugar (see Note)	8 ounces cherries, pitted and then
¼ cup brandy (optional)	pureed in a food processor until
1 teaspoon lemon juice, or to taste	smooth, plus more for garnish
1 teaspoon almond extract	Aged balsamic vinegar to garnish

Line two 9-inch loaf pans with plastic wrap, allowing it to overhang on all four sides.

Prepare an ice bath in a wide, shallow bowl or pan and set aside. Chill the bowl of a stand mixer and the wire whisk attachment, or a large metal bowl and the beaters of a hand mixer, by placing in the freezer.

Combine the egg yolks and sugar in a heatproof bowl and place over a pot of barely simmering water, making sure the bowl doesn't touch the surface of the water. Heat, whisking steadily, until the mixture melts into a thick liquid. Continue to whisk until it begins to form ribbons on the surface (about 4 minutes). Remove the bowl from the heat, place on the ice bath, and whisk until room temperature (about 3 minutes). Stir in the brandy (if using), lemon juice, and almond extract.

Using the chilled bowl and whisk attachment, or the chilled metal bowl and chilled beaters, whip the cream on high speed until it forms stiff peaks.

With a spatula, fold in the cherries, then fold in the egg yolk mixture. Pour the mixture into the prepared pan and cover with more plastic wrap to seal well.

Freeze for at least 8 hours, or ideally overnight. Remove the semifreddo from the freezer 20 to 30 minutes before serving so the rock-hard mixture can soften into an ice cream–like texture. Lift it out of the pan with the plastic wrap, then peel it off. Cut the semifreddo into 1½-inch-thick slices. Garnish each slice with aged balsamic and a few whole cherries. Serve immediately while still cold and partially frozen.

Variation

Cherry-Chocolate Semifreddo: For a decadent twist, fold finely chopped bittersweet chocolate (60% to 70% cacao) into the mixture before freezing. I use a generous ½ cup per loaf pan.

NOTE: *It's important to use superfine sugar for this so it will fully melt into the egg yolks. If you don't have any, you can make it by whizzing an equal amout of granulated sugar in a food processor for 1 to 2 minutes until very fine.*

Spumoni with Fresh Cherries
SERVES 8

This is a much more elegant, and really more Italian, version of the classic maraschino cherry and bright green pistachio ice cream dessert that became a staple of Italian American restaurants. It starts with a rich custard base lighted with rum-spiked whipped cream. Half gets studded with cherries and almonds, the other half gets blended with pistachios and orange zest. Then the two halves are layered, sliced, and served—no ice cream maker necessary. This was one of the most popular desserts at Genoa, and the recipe was a gift to owner Amelia Hard from the friendly folks at nearby Bread & Ink Café.

½ cup raw pistachios

½ cup raw slivered almonds

2 cups half-and-half

5 large egg yolks

¾ cup sugar

⅛ teaspoon salt

1 teaspoon pure vanilla extract

1 cup heavy cream

2 tablespoons dark rum

2 teaspoons almond extract

30 fresh cherries, pitted and halved

2 teaspoons orange zest

Preheat the oven to 350°F. Spread the pistachios on a baking sheet and toast for 8 to 10 minutes. Transfer to a plate to cool, then finely chop. Spread the almonds on the baking sheet and toast, 5 to 8 minutes. Transfer to another plate and allow to cool before finely chopping.

Line a 9-inch loaf pan (or another 8-cup capacity dish) with plastic wrap, allowing it to overhang on all four sides.

Bring the half-and-half almost to a simmer in a large saucepan over medium-low heat (bubbles should be forming around the sides of the pan). Meanwhile, whisk together the egg yolks, sugar, and salt in a medium bowl. Whisk about ½ cup of the hot liquid into the egg yolk mixture, then whisk this mixture back into the pan. Cook over low heat, stirring constantly, until the mixture reaches 175°F. Remove from the heat and stir in the vanilla. Transfer the custard to a bowl and allow to cool (to speed things up, nestle the bowl into a larger one filled with ice; stir the custard occasionally). Place a piece of plastic wrap directly on the surface to prevent a skin from forming, and refrigerate until cold. Can be made up to 3 days ahead.

Whip together the cream, rum, and almond extract in a large bowl until soft peaks form. Fold into the cold custard until thoroughly combined. Divide the mixture in half and fold the cherries and almonds into one portion. Fold the chopped pistachios and orange zest into the other and refrigerate. Spoon the cherry mixture into the prepared loaf pan, smooth the top, and freeze until beginning to firm up, about 1 hour. Spoon the pistachio mixture evenly on top of the cherry-almond layer. Freeze overnight, or until firm enough to slice.

To serve, use the plastic wrap to pull the frozen custard out of the pan. Invert the custard onto a serving platter and peel off the plastic wrap. Slice into ¾-inch-thick slices, let soften for a couple of minutes, then serve.

Bar Biscotti

MAKES 2 DOZEN

The bar at Nostrana is never without a tall vase of these crunchy, nutty dippers, which we purposely make dramatically long for maximum impact (after all, if you're going to serve cookies at a bar, they should have some personality). They're also big on almond flavor, almost too much, but that's what makes them so addictive. You can't help but fall in love with that bitter almond flavor. They're great dipped in wine or coffee, and they make a lovely snack, too. The recipe came to us via acclaimed chef Marda Stoliar, who has spent decades teaching countless people how to open bakeries from her cooking school in Bend, Oregon. I went to her for help dialing in my pizza dough and left with a biscotti recipe in the bargain.

1 cup sliced or whole almonds

¾ cup hazelnuts (roasted and skins removed) or pecans

8 tablespoons (1 stick) plus 1 tablespoon unsalted butter, at room temperature

1¼ cups sugar

3 cups pastry flour

2 large eggs

1¾ teaspoons almond extract

½ teaspoon anise extract

¼ teaspoon fine sea salt

2 teaspoons baking powder

Preheat the oven to 300°F. Line one baking sheet with parchment paper.

Arrange the almonds and hazelnuts in a single layer on the prepared baking sheet. Toast for about 15 minutes, stirring occasionally, until they barely start to turn color. This step is mainly to dry out the nuts. They will deepen in color and flavor when baking the biscotti.

Remove from the oven and allow the nuts to cool, then coarsely chop them together in a food processor or nut grinder, allowing some nuts to remain whole, others chopped fine, and most medium-chopped. Keep the parchment on the baking sheet, to reuse when baking the biscotti.

Increase the oven temperature to 350°F.

Cream together the butter, sugar, and 1¼ cups of the pastry flour at medium speed in a stand mixer fitted with the paddle attachment until light, about 10 minutes. Alternatively, cream the mixture in a large bowl, using an electric hand mixer.

Add the eggs, one at a time, beating for 2 minutes after each addition and stopping to scrape down the sides of the bowl. Beat in the almond and anise extracts, then scrape down the sides of the bowl.

Add the remaining 1¾ cups of pastry flour, salt, baking powder, and nuts. Pulse the mixer on and off to quickly mix in the flour, stopping as soon as no crumbles remain on the bottom of the mixing bowl.

Transfer the dough to the prepared baking sheet. Squeeze and shape the dough into two logs the width of the baking sheet at least 6 inches apart. The logs should be about 1 inch high by 2 inches wide. Allowing the ends of the logs to touch the sides of the pan will help keep them uniformly shaped during baking. If you need to move the logs, gently roll them, rather than picking them up.

Bake the logs for 20 to 30 minutes, until they are very light brown, the tops have cracked down the middle from end to end, and they feel semifirm. Remove from the oven and lower the temperature to 200°F.

Allow the logs to cool until just warm, about 25 minutes. Use a long, nonserrated knife, slice the logs diagonally, ¾ inch thick, starting at the center of each log. (It helps to think about positioning your knife at a 10 o'clock to 4 o'clock angle as you go.)

Place the biscotti, cut side up, on the baking sheet, leaving ½ inch between each slice. Return the pan to the oven and bake for 45 minutes to 1 hour, until hard. The second bake does not have to occur immediately; it can be delayed up to 3 hours after slicing.

Turn off the oven and leave the biscotti inside for another hour, propping the door open slightly with a wooden spoon. To test for doneness, press the cut side of the cookies; they should feel very hard with no give. If necessary, reheat the oven to 200°F and bake for a little longer.

Piedmontese Baked Peaches
WITH AMARETTI AND CACAO
SERVES 4 TO 8

ⵏⵏⵏ

There's a reason that peaches and almonds go so perfectly together. Tucked inside a peach pit is a diminutive kernel that looks a lot like an almond, not because of some fluke of nature, but because peaches and almonds are cousins. And that kernel is a source of intense and highly prized bitter almond flavor, like almond extract but in its natural form. In fact, in this classic dessert found in trattorias throughout the Piedmont region, the kernel often gets chopped up and mixed with amaretti cookies to create a double-almond filling for fresh peaches baked until warm and soft. I think amaretti are flavorful enough, so this version skips that laborious step, but feel free to hammer your peach pits open if you like. Piedmontese Moscato d'Asti is a classic pairing, but the addition of cocoa powder adds a note of gravitas that allows the dish to pair just as wonderfully with a light-bodied red. Add a dollop of ice cream or whipped cream and savor the warm-cool contrast.

4 large, ripe, sweet, freestone peaches

2 tablespoons sugar

Eight 2-inch amaretti cookies, crushed

2½ tablespoons unsalted butter, at room temperature, plus more for buttering the dish

1 large egg yolk, at room temperature

1 teaspoon Dutch-processed unsweetened cocoa powder, preferably Valrhona brand

Crème fraîche, mascarpone, or ice cream for serving (optional)

Preheat oven to 350°F. Butter a 9-by-13-inch baking dish.

Cut the peaches in half around the equator and twist to separate; wiggle the pit to loosen and discard. Carve out the center of the peach to make a slightly larger hollow (about the diameter of a golf ball) and finely chop the removed flesh.

Combine the chopped peach with the sugar, half of the amaretti cookie crumbs, butter, egg yolk, and cocoa powder in a small bowl.

Place the peach halves in the baking dish and fill each with a mound of the amaretti mixture. Sprinkle the remaining amaretti on top.

Bake until the peaches are soft, about 45 minutes. Serve warm alone or topped with crème fraîche, mascarpone, or ice cream (vanilla or almond would complement nicely).

Summer Fruit Crisp
WITH ALMOND CREAM
SERVES 6 TO 8

Even if you claim not to be a baker, you can absolutely execute this wonderful dessert. That's what tops the long list of its many attributes, along with how happily it accommodates any fruit in any season, uses pantry staples everyone has on hand, takes minutes to make, requires no special equipment, and everyone loves it. At Nostrana, we always have this crisp on the menu, baked to order and with fruit that changes from day to day depending on what our farmers bring us. But one thing remains constant: It's always served with a spoonful of almond cream. The recipe, which makes about two cups and requires a three-hour steep, comes from March, a fabulous Manhattan restaurant (sadly no longer in business), by way of Kathryn Yeomans, Nostrana's opening head chef, who worked there before she joined our kitchen. Similar in texture to a crème Anglaise, almond cream is so versatile that you'll find plenty of destinations for it, including drizzled onto fresh fruit or as a creamy pool underneath a slice of cake. It's the finishing touch that takes this from simple to sublime.

ALMOND CREAM

4 ounces (¾ cup) whole unblanched almonds

¼ cup plus 2 tablespoons sugar, or ¼ cup mild honey

2 cups heavy cream

Tiny pinch of salt

⅛ teaspoon bitter almond extract (see Note), or ¼ teaspoon almond extract

SUMMER FRUIT CRISP

8 tablespoons (1 stick) cold unsalted butter, cut into small pieces, plus more for buttering pan

4 cups mixed fresh soft fruits in season, such as berries, chopped figs, currants, sliced stone fruits, and pitted cherries

¾ cup (90 g) all-purpose flour

¾ cup sugar

½ teaspoon salt

TO MAKE THE ALMOND CREAM

Line a large strainer with a couple of layers of cheesecloth and set over a bowl.

Combine the almonds and sugar in a food processor and process until the almonds are finely ground, about 2 minutes.

continues

Meanwhile, heat the cream in a medium saucepan over medium heat until quite warm but not yet boiling. Remove from the heat and add the ground almond mixture and the pinch of salt. Let the almonds and cream steep for about 3 hours to infuse the cream with plenty of almond flavor.

Strain the cream through the cheesecloth, pressing on the nut solids to extract as much flavor as possible. Stir in the bitter almond extract, taste, and add a touch more if you like. Refrigerate the cream until cold.

TO MAKE THE SUMMER FRUIT CRISP

Preheat the oven to 375°F. Butter a deep 9-inch pie plate or 8-by-8-inch baking dish.

Wash, peel, seed/pit, and slice/chop the fruit as necessary (small berries and cherries can be left whole). Arrange the fruit evenly in the baking dish.

Combine the flour, sugar, and salt in a food processor or stand mixer. Add the butter and pulse or mix until the mixture resembles coarse cornmeal in texture, taking care not to blend the butter too thoroughly. Alternatively, grate the butter on the large holes of a box grater and work into the flour mixture with your fingertips. Scatter the topping evenly over the fruit. Tap the dish on the counter once or twice to settle in the crumbs.

Bake on the top rack of the oven (to encourage browning) until the topping is golden brown, the juices are bubbling, and the fruit is tender when pierced with a skewer, 35 to 45 minutes (it could take longer depending on the size of the fruit pieces). Serve warm with a generous lashing of Almond Cream.

• •

NOTE: *Bitter almond extract is sold at specialty stores, including online through King Arthur Baking Company.*

Olive Oil Cake
(TORTA ALL'OLIO D'OLIVE)
SERVES 8

● ●

This easy cake is certainly nothing fancy, but sometimes it's the homey desserts that make the biggest impression. Whether served alone or with a fluffy spoonful of cream and some fruit, it's a soul-satisfying finish to any meal and a wonderful showcase for olive oil—particularly Tuscan olive oils, with their grassy, peppery flavors that pair exceedingly well with the cake's jammy raisins and juicy tangerines. I think what I love most, though, is that it comes from Dario Cecchini, the most famous butcher in the world and a friend we brought to Portland many times over the years for an annual butcher event in the wine country called Maialata. If you go to Dario's famed butcher shop, Antica Macelleria Cecchini in Panzano, Tuscany (and you definitely should), check out the picture of us all hung on the wall—then visit one of his nearby restaurants where you can enjoy a slice of this cake, too.

¼ cup golden raisins

¼ cup plus 1 tablespoon vin santo

1¼ cups sugar, plus more for dusting

2 large eggs, at room temperature

1 large egg yolk, at room temperature

½ cup plus 2 tablespoons flavorful extra-virgin olive oil, plus more for oiling pan

2¼ cups (270 g) all-purpose flour

1 tablespoon baking powder

2 teaspoons sea salt

3 small thin-skinned tangerines or small oranges, or 1 navel orange

¼ cup plus 1 tablespoon water

2 teaspoons pure vanilla extract

¼ cup sparkling sugar for the top (granulated sugar will work, too)

Softly whipped cream or mascarpone and fresh stone fruit, fruit compote, poached fruit, or preserves for serving (optional)

Preheat the oven to 350°F. Combine the raisins and vin santo in a small bowl and allow to soak for at least 30 minutes (you can warm the mixture, if you like, so the liquid gets absorbed faster).

Whisk together the sugar, eggs, and egg yolk in a large mixing bowl until well combined and pale yellow in color, about 2 minutes by hand. Whisk in the olive oil until blended.

Combine the flour, baking powder, and salt in a medium bowl. (If you want the raisins to bake inside the cake rather than on top, add them to the flour mixture and toss. Reserve any liquid that didn't get absorbed and add to the cake later.)

Cut the peel off the top and bottom of the tangerines. Stand them on one end and cut along the sides to remove the peel. Lay each piece flat with the white pith exposed and use your knife to shave the pith away, then finely chop the zest. Add the zest to the flour mixture. Cut the fruit in half, remove the seeds, and chop finely. Place the fruit and any juices in a large measuring cup. You should have ¾ cup (adjust with more or less fruit as needed). Stir in any leftover vin santo, the water, and the vanilla.

Alternate adding the flour mixture and tangerine mixture to the egg mixture, starting and ending with the flour mixture.

Lightly coat a 9-inch round cake pan with olive oil and dust with sugar, tapping out the excess. Pour the batter into the pan. If you haven't already added the raisins, sprinkle on top and use an offset spatula to cover with batter. Sprinkle the cake evenly with the sparkling sugar. Bake for 50 minutes, until golden and a toothpick inserted in the center comes out clean and dry.

Remove from the oven and allow to cool for 10 minutes before removing from the pan and cooling completely on a rack. Serve alone or with a garnish of softly whipped cream or mascarpone and fresh stone fruit, fruit compote, poached fruit, or preserves.

Seasonal Olive Oil

Italians often take a seasonal approach to their olive oil. When the olives are harvested and processed in fall, usually late October and early November, the resulting oil, called *olio nuovo*, has robust, grassy, and piquant flavor notes, even when made with a mild variety of olives. That bold flavor is an ideal match for the beefy braises, bitter chicories, and woodsy mushrooms of fall and winter. But as those volatile molecules age, the oil mellows in flavor. By summer, when delicate stone fruits, juicy tomatoes, tender lettuces, and crisp cucumbers make their appearance on the table, the oil has mellowed into a buttery richness that won't overpower their flavors.

GCBC (Garlic Chile Bread Crumbs)

MAKES ABOUT 1 CUP

We always have these crumbs on hand to be able to add a crunchy, spicy layer to a range of dishes—pastas, salads, stuffed zucchini flowers, stuffed peppers coming out bubbling straight from the wood oven (hungry yet?) . . . any dish that wants some textural contrast.

For the best bread crumbs, start with good bread. I usually use focaccia, but any artisan bread will do. If you're using a soft-crusted loaf, no need to cut off the crust, but for loaves that have crustier exteriors, slice off most of it and just use the interior crumb. I use three varieties of dried chili powder in this condiment because I love the complexity, but the crumbs will still be delicious and spunky with just one or two chili powders and the paprika.

1 cup fresh bread crumbs

2 tablespoons extra-virgin olive oil

1 tablespoon Controne pepper

1 tablespoon Espelette pepper

1 tablespoon cayenne pepper

1 tablespoon sweet paprika

3 garlic cloves, grated or mashed into a pulp

Pinch of sea salt

Preheat the oven to 350°F. Toss the bread crumbs and olive oil in a bowl until the oil is fully distributed. Spread the crumbs on a baking sheet and toast in the oven until crisp, dry, and light golden, about 8 minutes. Remove from the oven and let the crumbs cool.

Toss the toasted bread crumbs with the three powdered peppers, paprika, garlic, and salt. Keep tossing until the garlic is fully distributed.

Use right away or store in an airtight container at room temperature for up to 2 weeks.

Salsa Verde

MAKES 1 CUP

● ●

With its pop of vinegar and salty anchovies, this herby condiment can stand up to more intense flavors, which is why it's the traditional way to gussy up bollito misto, the ancient Piedmontese cavalcade of boiled meats and offal. But zingy, zesty salsa verde can liven up just about anything, from roasted potatoes or cauliflower to grilled meats or fish, such as tuna or swordfish. When you want an enhancement that lets the food speak for itself, Salmoriglio (page 170) is the way to go. When you want a condiment that throws a punch, look no further.

One 2-inch-thick slice artisan bread, crust removed

2 tablespoons red wine vinegar

1 cup loosely packed fresh flat-leaf parsley leaves

3 oil-packed anchovy fillets

2 garlic cloves

Generous pinch of red pepper flakes

Yolk of 1 large hard-boiled egg (see Agliata, page 116)

½ cup extra-virgin olive oil

Sea salt

Place the bread in a small bowl and drizzle with the red wine vinegar. Allow to sit for 10 minutes. Roughly chop the parsley, anchovies, and garlic, and place the mixture in a food processor. Add the bread, red pepper flakes, and egg yolk. Process to a uniform mixture. Stir in the olive oil and season with salt to taste. Serve at room temperature.

Salmoriglio

MAKES ¾ CUP

So simple, so Sicilian—and so versatile. Composed of olive oil, lemon juice, oregano, and a touch of garlic, this sauce can enhance so many things. It's lovely on grilled or poached fish, lamb or chicken, or grilled summer vegetables, such as eggplant, zucchini, mushrooms, and even grilled onions or scallions. It can even be used as a marinade. It's bursting with bright, herby flavor and perfect for almost anything you're cooking this summer. Because it relies heavily on lemon juice, it's best to make it fresh the day you plan to use it. Lemon juice loses its sunny brightness as it sits, becoming more harshly acidic instead. That's why the bartenders at Nostrana are always tasting their lemon juice over the course of the night. Luckily, there's no need to make this ahead, as it takes mere minutes to mix up from start to finish.

1 cup loosely packed fresh flat-leaf parsley leaves

¼ cup loosely packed fresh oregano leaves

3 tablespoons salted capers (rinsed, soaked in cold water for 10 minutes, then drained)

2 tablespoons fresh mint (optional)

1 garlic clove, minced

Zest of 1 lemon

Juice of 1 or 2 lemons

½ cup extra-virgin olive oil, or more as needed

Sea salt and freshly ground black pepper

Combine the parsley, oregano, capers, mint, and garlic in a blender or food processor (see Note) and pulse until finely chopped. Add the lemon zest and juice (start with the juice of 1 lemon and add more later, if desired). With the machine running, add the olive oil and blend until emulsified and creamy. Season with salt and pepper to taste. Add more lemon juice or olive oil, if desired.

NOTE: *If you don't have a food processor, you can chop every ingredient finely and whisk with olive oil and lemon juice in a bowl.*

Salsa Piccante

MAKES 1½ CUPS

Capers, olives, and red pepper flakes lift this bold and herby sauce out of pesto territory and into a league of its own. It adds so much oomph to simple baked, grilled, or poached fish, but it's also wonderful mixed with potato salad, tuna salad, or smoky vegetables hot off the grill.

⅓ cup plus 1 tablespoon pine nuts, untoasted

1 cup chopped fresh flat-leaf parsley leaves

¼ cup fine fresh bread crumbs

2 tablespoons capers, rinsed and drained

¾ cup pitted brined black olives, such as Gaeta or Kalamata or Taggiasca (about ¾ cup)

2 garlic cloves

¾ cup extra-virgin olive oil

2 tablespoons freshly squeezed lemon juice

1½ tablespoons sherry vinegar

¾ teaspoon red pepper flakes

Sea salt and freshly ground black pepper

Combine the pine nuts, parsley, bread crumbs, capers, olives, and garlic in a food processor and pulse into a coarse paste. Pour in half of the olive oil and process into a fine paste. With the machine running, pour in the remaining oil, lemon juice, and vinegar until emulsified. Season to taste with red pepper flakes, salt, and black pepper.

BONUS
Salsa Piccante Muffaletta

SERVES 2 TO 4

Salsa piccante always reminds me of the sweet-sour olive salad that traditionally goes on a muffaletta. Even the texture of the classic muffaletta bread reminds me of focaccia. So, it makes sense to use these classic Italian staples to make an Italian version of the New Orleans staple. It has Italian roots, after all—the creator was a deli owner who emigrated from Sicily. The sandwich tastes best when given time to allow the juices to soak into the bread, making this an ideal make-ahead sandwich to take along on a picnic.

½ sheet Focaccia (page 90)

1 batch Salsa Piccante (page 171)

5 ounces thinly sliced salumi, such as sopressata

5 ounces thinly sliced cold cuts, such as mortadella

5 ounces thinly sliced cured whole meats, such as coppa or prosciutto

5 ounces fresh mozzarella or young provolone

Split the focaccia in half horizontally. Spread the cut sides generously with salsa piccante.

Layer the meats and cheese on the bottom focaccia slice, alternating as you would to construct lasagna. Top with the remaining slice of focaccia, wrap tightly in plastic wrap to compress the sandwich, and let rest at room temperature for 1 hour before cutting into quarters, then cutting each quarter diagonally and serving.

Eggplant Puree
(CREMA DI MELANZÁNE)
MAKES ABOUT 2 CUPS

A hint of smoke, a spritz of lemon, and a generous helping of garlic transform mild eggplant into a pungent puree that's a lovely dip for raw or grilled vegetables or crostini (see page 4).

2 large eggplants (2 pounds total), tops trimmed, halved

⅓ cup high-quality extra-virgin olive oil, plus more for brushing the eggplants

¼ cup freshly squeezed lemon juice

Fine sea salt

White pepper

4 garlic cloves, smashed into a paste

Prepare a charcoal grill for direct cooking over medium heat (350° to 400°F). Scrub the cooking grates clean. Brush the cut sides of the eggplants with olive oil. Place the eggplant halves, cut side down, on the grill and cook with the lid on until browned and beginning to soften, about 15 minutes. Turn over and continue cooking until soft all the way through, about 15 minutes more. Remove from the heat.

When cool enough to handle, remove any long strands of seeds. Scoop the flesh into a food processor and discard the skins. Puree the eggplant until smooth, then blend in the olive oil and the lemon juice. Season with salt and pepper to taste. Transfer to a bowl and stir in the garlic. Taste and add more salt, pepper, lemon juice, olive oil, and garlic, if desired. The mixture should taste almost aggressively flavorful because the flavors will mellow after chilling (the garlic, however, will get more pungent after a couple of days). Cover and chill. Serve the puree on a grilled vegetable platter or on its own, surrounded by crostini.

Basil Pesto
WITH VARIATIONS
MAKES ABOUT 1 CUP

• •

Liguria is famous for its basil, and it's not just the region's terroir and proximity to the sea breezes of the Italian Riviera that justify this fame. It's also the strict attention to detail when growing it. The best, DOP-certified Ligurian basil is grown for only about 28 days and picked when still young and tender, making it ideal for pounding into bright green pesto alla Geno-vese. Buying basil in Liguria is like buying bundles of delicate plant starts—far different from the lush bunches of large mature leaves we buy here in the States. That's why I recommend taking the extra step of briefly blanching basil for pesto. It helps tenderize the leaves and sets their bright color, allowing them to be pureed without bruising and turning a murky shade of brown. After all, the vibrant green color is so much a part of the pesto experience.

I often make big batches of pesto each summer and freeze it for use all year long. There's nothing nicer than knowing you have a stash of it just waiting to garnish a soup, coat a bowl-ful of gnocchi, or top a pizza. When making pesto to freeze (see Note), I omit the garlic and Parmesan, and instead wait to add them to the defrosted pesto before using. Garlic tends to taste oddly strong when frozen, and freezing cheese turns it rubbery.

Sea salt

2 cups tightly packed fresh basil leaves

⅓ cup pine nuts, lightly toasted and cooled

2 garlic cloves, finely chopped

½ to ¾ cup extra-virgin olive oil, or more as needed

1 cup finely grated Parmigiano-Reggiano

Freshly ground black pepper

Bring a large pot of water to a boil over high heat. Add a generous pinch of salt. Set a large bowl of ice water nearby.

Drop the basil leaves into the boiling water, stir, then remove the leaves with a spider or slotted spoon and plunge immediately into the ice water. Keep them submerged by

continues

pressing down with the spider. Remove the basil from the ice water, leaving behind any ice, and squeeze dry.

Pulse the pine nuts in a food processor until finely chopped. Add the basil and garlic and pulse until combined. With the machine running, pour in ½ cup of the olive oil and process until a smooth, bright green paste forms, stopping to scrape the sides as needed. Stir in more oil if you want a looser texture.

Transfer the pesto to a bowl, stir in the Parmesan, and season with salt and pepper.

● ●

NOTE: *If freezing the pesto, omit the garlic and Parmesan. Transfer the pesto to a sealable container, smooth the surface, and pour a layer of olive oil on top to protect the surface from air. Freeze. When ready to use, allow the pesto to defrost and then stir in the garlic, smashed into a paste, and the grated Parmesan.*

VARIATION
Arugula Pesto
MAKES 1 CUP

Peppery arugula doesn't have the same tendency to bruise, so there's no need to blanch the leaves before using. And since arugula is its prime in late spring and early summer, this is the pesto to make when you're waiting for basil to hit the farmers' market.

Follow the recipe for classic Basil Pesto, skipping the blanching step and pureeing 4 loosely packed cups of regular or baby arugula leaves instead of the basil.

Basil, Hazelnut, and Ricotta Pesto
MAKES 1 CUP

I like cooking with hazelnuts because they are such an Oregon treasure. They're also a highly prized nut from Piemonte, my favorite region of Italy, and find their way into many traditional Piedmontese dishes at Nostrana. In this recipe, hazelnuts stand in for pine nuts, offering a more robustly nutty flavor that can stand up to the richness of ricotta and butter. This makes a wonderful room temperature sauce for salmon, halibut, tuna, chicken breasts, and, of course, fettuccine and potato gnocchi.

¼ cup hazelnuts, lightly toasted, skins rubbed off

2 cups tightly packed fresh basil leaves

2 garlic cloves, finely chopped

⅓ to ½ cup extra-virgin olive oil

½ cup finely grated Parmigiano-Reggiano cheese

3 tablespoons fresh or Homemade Ricotta (page 189), preferably made with sheep's milk

2 tablespoons unsalted butter, softened

Sea salt

Pulse the hazelnuts in a food processor until finely chopped. Add the basil and garlic and pulse again. With the machine running, slowly pour in enough olive oil to create a smooth, bright green paste (you may not need it all), stopping to scrape the sides as needed.

Transfer the pesto to a bowl. Stir in the Parmesan, ricotta, and butter, and season with salt.

Aioli

MAKES 2 CUPS

€ €

This garlicky mayonnaise is so flavorful it can be used as a dip for raw vegetables or roasted potatoes, or as a sauce for anything that could use a dollop of creamy garlicky goodness. Although the name is French, historians say the ancient Romans likely invented it, and that's Italian enough for me. The secret to aioli is to add the oil very, very slowly so that it will emulsify with the egg yolk and lemon juice. If it ends up too stiff and thick, whisk in a little water to thin it out.

2 garlic cloves

Sea salt

2 large egg yolks

¼ teaspoon dry mustard

2 cups fruity (not grassy) extra-virgin olive oil

Juice of 1 lemon

Pound the garlic and salt into a smooth paste with a mortar and pestle. Alternatively, chop the garlic, sprinkle with salt, then use the flat side of your knife to crush the garlic and salt into a smooth paste, then scrape the garlic paste into a bowl and use a whisk to incorporate the next ingredients.

Mix in the egg yolks and mustard. Slowly mix in ¼ cup of the olive oil, drop by drop, until the mixture is thick, creamy, and emulsified. (This is a slow process. Don't be tempted to speed it up. You will be rewarded soon.) If using a pestle, change to using a whisk at this point. Whisk in half of the lemon juice and then whisk in the olive oil, drop by drop, until the mixture is very thick again. Repeat the process of adding lemon juice and olive oil until each is completely incorporated. If the mixture is too thick and stiff, thin it out by whisking in a little water. Add salt to taste.

NOTE: *If you don't want an arm workout, you can blend the aioli in a food processor, but take care with the oil. High-speed blending can sometimes encourage olive oil to contribute bitter compounds to a mixture, which is especially obvious in sauces that are mostly extra-virgin olive oil, as this one is. Instead, try using 1 cup of neutral vegetable oil, such as sunflower, for the initial blending. One the mixture is emulsified, whisk in 1 cup of olive oil by hand.*

Green Goddess Dressing

This creamy, jade-hued dressing has a wonderfully fresh and herby flavor and works perfectly on tender little gem and butter lettuces. But it's not just for salads. Try serving it alongside crudités, grilled vegetables, fritto misto, simple grilled fish, or even fried oysters.

1 cup fresh flat-leaf parsley leaves

1 cup fresh basil leaves

2 scallions, white and light green parts only, chopped roughly

3 tablespoons roughly chopped chives

1 garlic clove, chopped roughly

2 anchovy fillets, preferably salt-packed, rinsed, soaked, and filleted (see page xiv)

¼ cup freshly squeezed lemon juice

½ cup extra-virgin olive oil

¼ cup Aioli (page 178), homemade mayonnaise, or Duke's brand

¼ cup sour cream

Sea salt and freshly ground black pepper

Puree the parsley, basil, scallions, chives, garlic, anchovies, lemon juice, and olive oil in a blender until smooth. Add the aioli and sour cream and blend again until smooth. Season with salt and pepper to taste.

Summery Tomato Sauce

MAKES ABOUT 3 CUPS

Adding just a touch of onion, garlic, and basil enhances the fresh sun-ripened juiciness of summer tomatoes without overwhelming their flavor. The result is a sauce that's light and fresh and lively—and happy to be paired with any pasta you choose.

3 tablespoons extra-virgin olive oil

1 large spring onion, chopped

1 garlic clove, minced

6 medium tomatoes, peeled, seeded, and chopped (see How To Peel Tomatoes, page 181), or one 28-ounce can whole peeled San Marzano tomatoes

Sea salt and freshly ground black pepper

8 fresh basil sprigs, leaves torn

Pinch of sugar, if needed

Heat the oil in a large, deep sauté pan or Dutch oven over medium-low heat. Add the spring onion and garlic and sauté slowly until soft, about 15 minutes, keeping an eye on the heat level to keep the ingredients from burning.

Add the tomatoes and their juices (if using whole canned tomatoes, crush with your hands as you add them to the pot). Season with a generous pinch of salt and a few grindings of pepper. Cook, stirring often, until the mixture thickens, about 30 minutes. Stir in the basil and taste. Season with a little sugar if the sauce seems too tart, or more salt if it seems dull. Puree in a blender, or use an immersion blender, if desired. Use with your favorite pasta or in casseroles such as Zucchini Parmigiana (page 104).

How to Peel Tomatoes

To peel tomatoes, bring a pot of water to a boil over high heat and place a bowl of ice water nearby. Score an X in the bottom of each tomato. Lower into the water and boil for 1 to 2 minutes, until the skin at the X begins to loosen. Remove with a slotted spoon and plunge into the ice water to stop the cooking. When cool enough to handle, peel away the skins, which should come off easily.

If you want to remove the seeds without using a food mill, cut the tomatoes in half and squeeze out the seeds and juices into a sieve set over a bowl. Discard the seeds. Coarsely chop the tomato flesh and add to the recipe along with the juices.

Marcella Hazan's Tomato Butter Sauce

MAKES 2½ CUPS; SERVES 4 TO 6

This famous sauce has been heaped with praise for decades, and it deserves every bit of it. Just stew fresh or canned tomatoes with a halved onion and a stick of butter, and the result is the ne plus ultra of tomato sauces—luscious and rich without tasting jammy or overcooked. It's somehow both light and fresh, deep and savory, which is why it's one of the few sauces that works as well with dried pastas as it does with fresh, and even gnocchi.

Although there's almost zero prep work when using canned tomatoes, the sauce is extraordinary when made with fresh. We use a bit more butter than the original, but the real secret is to simmer the sauce long enough for the fat to separate and float on top. That's when you know the water has boiled away and the tomatoes are fully concentrated.

One 28-ounce can Italian plum tomatoes (preferably San Marzano), or 2 pounds fresh ripe plum tomatoes, peeled (see "How to Peel Tomatoes," page 181)

8 tablespoons (1 stick) unsalted butter

1 medium onion, peeled, root end slightly trimmed but kept intact, cut in half

Pinch of sugar

Flaky sea salt

Crush the tomatoes with your hands as you add them to a medium saucepan. If using canned tomatoes, add the juice as well.

Add the butter, onion, and sugar, and season with salt. Cook at a slow but steady simmer, uncovered, until the fat separates from tomatoes, about 45 minutes.

Discard the onion (or eat it—it's delicious!), taste the sauce, and add salt, if necessary. Toss with the pasta or gnocchi of your choice.

Basic Fresh Pasta

MAKES 1 POUND; SERVES 4 TO 6

● ● ● ●● ● ● ● ● ● ● ● ● ● ●● ● ● ● ●● ● ● ●● ● ● ● ● ● ● ●● ● ●● ● ● ●

This recipe is an ideal starting point built on a classic ratio of flour to egg that produces a pasta stretchy enough to be rolled and filled without tearing, while the splash of cream makes it tender enough to taste like a luxury. It's a trick I learned from Patricia Wells's wonderful cookbook *The Food Lover's Guide to Paris*. However, I skip the cream when using the dough for noodles, so they'll have a chewier texture. This is an easy recipe to memorize, and you'll probably find making fresh pasta is really quite fun, in which case a hand-cranked pasta machine will soon become your favorite tool in the kitchen.

2½ cups (300 g) all-purpose flour

3 large eggs

3 tablespoons heavy cream (if using the dough for ravioli; otherwise omit)

1½ teaspoons sea salt (if using the dough for ravioli; otherwise omit)

Semola rimacinata (see page xx) for sprinkling

Place the flour in a mound on a clean, dry, wooden work surface or in the bottom of a large bowl. Make a well in the center. Crack the eggs into the well and use a fork to break them up and whisk them together. Add the cream and salt, if using. Begin to gradually whisk in the flour, pushing it in bit by bit from the edges, until you have a shaggy mixture.

Use your hands to knead the dough into a cohesive mass. Continue to knead, pushing out against the dough with the bottom of your palm, folding it over back onto itself, turning a smidge to the right and repeating, over and over, until it's smooth and pliable, at least 10 minutes. If the dough still seems sticky after a few minutes of kneading, sprinkle with a little semola flour. If it seems dry and cracking, wet your hands and continue kneading.

Wrap in plastic, shape into a disk, and allow to rest at room temperature for at least 1 hour, or refrigerate for a longer rest. The dough can be refrigerated for up to 3 days.

TO ROLL OUT THE DOUGH WITH A PASTA MACHINE

Divide the pasta dough into quarters. Work with one quarter at a time and keep the rest covered with plastic wrap. Flatten and mold one quarter of the pasta into a rectangular shape, then pass it through the largest setting on a pasta machine. Fold the edges of the

continues

emerged sheet inward so the edges are touching, then fold the entire sheet in half like a book. Feed it through the machine, narrow edge first. Repeat the folding and rolling procedure one more time.

Adjust the rollers to the next setting and roll the pasta through, catching it with one hand as it comes out. Continue to roll the pasta through each consecutively tighter setting until the sheet is as thin as desired. Tip: Turn the crank slowly and try to keep the pasta as wide as the roller. If the sheet is getting too long and unwieldy, feel free to cut it in half and roll each half separately.

TO MAKE RAVIOLI
See Shrimp Ravioli in Brodo (page 82).

TO MAKE NOODLES
Pass the sheet through the cutting attachment on the pasta machine. Or dust the pasta sheet thoroughly with semola flour and fold in half, fold in half on itself twice more, then use a sharp knife or pizza cutter to slice it into ribbons (¼ inch for fettuccine, ½ inch for pappardelle). Unfold and drape the noodles on a pasta drying rack or lay on a baking sheet dusted generously in semola flour to keep the pasta from sticking.

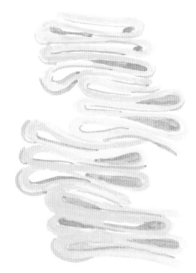

TO SERVE
Bring a large pot of salted water to a gentle rolling boil. Add the pasta and boil gently for 1 to 3 minutes, depending on the thickness. Remove with a slotted spoon as the noodles finish cooking and slide into warmed sauce.

Fresh Pasta Perfection

Silky, tender, and pleasantly springy, fresh pasta always feels extra special, even though it's just a simple mixture of flour and eggs (or flour and water, in the case of pici). But as with all elemental recipes, the fewer the ingredients, the more those ingredients—and how you handle them—matter.

First, use good, fresh, pasture-raised eggs, the kind that have bright orange yolks. This will ensure pasta with a lovely golden hue and richer flavor. You can even go all out and add a bunch of egg yolks to the mix (and a little more flour) for a richer, eggy variation.

As for the flour, all-purpose works perfectly well and results in a classic and versatile pasta, or you can go in a heartier direction by mixing in some whole wheat flour or semola rimacinata, which is a fine-milled semola flour. Want something more delicate? Use finely milled 00 flour. I prefer mixing these specialty flours with all-purpose for a more balanced variation, but you can go all the way if you like.

Some recipes add olive oil, but I don't since it can keep the gluten from forming (the gluten is what gives the pasta a spring in its step). And I don't bother salting the dough since I salt the cooking water generously. But I do think it's fun to get fancy with pureed herbs or vegetables for eye-popping color and flavor.

Your first foray into fresh pasta making might feel intimidating, especially since there are all sorts of variables that can affect the texture of your dough, from the humidity of your kitchen to the precise amount of egg that was in the shell. But don't stress: Fresh pasta is not only infinitely customizable, it's also forgiving. Just mix the wet and dry ingredients and knead for a good 10 minutes, or until the gluten develops and the pasta feels smooth, adding a little more flour if it seems wet or sticky, or sprinkling with some water if it seems crumbly or prone to cracking. Be sure to let the dough rest for a minimum of 1 hour for the gluten to relax and the flour to hydrate evenly.

Rolled-out dough desperately wants to stick to itself and every surface it touches, so keep a bag of semola rimacinata at the ready. It has the texture of fine cornmeal, which is great for coating the pasta and preventing sticking, but it hydrates in the boiling water like regular flour, so you won't end up with tough crunchy bits in your pasta.

Perfect Beans

MAKES 6 TO 7 CUPS

Beans might not be the first thing that comes to mind when you think of summery dishes, but they're actually your best friend when the weather heats up. Cook a big pot, and you can have a week's worth of light yet protein-rich lunches and dinners without ever having to turn on the oven or stove again. You can toss them into grain salads, mash them into sandwich fillings and dips, or serve them on their own, drizzled with vinaigrette and tossed with flavorful ingredients, such as tuna and pickled vegetables (see Cannellini Bean and Grilled Tuna Salad with Giardiniera, page 38).

Although there are countless methods and tips for cooking beans, they're actually pretty hard to mess up. Still, for the most luscious, plump, perfectly cooked beans, it's best to take a low and slow approach. I soak them overnight, which helps them cook more evenly, and then I bake them in the oven, which provides gentle, allover heat to ensure each bean turns out tender and creamy. Just be sure not to add anything acidic, such as lemon juice or tomatoes, until the end of cooking, as acid can toughen the skins and keep the beans from softening.

Of course, there are quicker methods, but this is a set-it-and-forget-it approach that will never fail, and the aromatics add subtle flavor perfect for every bean recipe in this book and beyond.

1 pound dried beans, rinsed and picked over for any stones or dirt clods

1 teaspoon salt, plus more for soaking beans

1 dried red chile pepper

6 garlic cloves, peeled

1 large sage sprig

1 bay leaf

3 tablespoons extra-virgin olive oil

Combine the beans and a generous pinch of salt in a heavy enameled cast-iron or clay bean pot. Add enough water to cover by 3 inches. Soak for at least 8 hours or overnight in the refrigerator or at cool room temperature.

Preheat the oven to 200°F. Drain the beans, return them to the pot, and add enough water to cover by 2 inches. Stir in the chile pepper, garlic, sage, bay leaf, the teaspoon of salt, and olive oil. Cover the pot and place it in the oven.

Bake for 3 to 8 hours, depending on the size and variety of bean and how fresh they are. Start testing the beans for doneness every hour after 3 hours. They're done when tender all the way through but not falling apart. Remove from the oven and let sit for 15 minutes before salting to taste. If you have time, allow to cool and refrigerate overnight before using, for the creamiest texture. Cooked beans will keep for 5 days refrigerated.

Il Fagioli

Like tomatoes, beans are a New World crop that have since become integral to Italian cuisine, which is why there are so many interesting varieties to play with. In fact, beans are so common in the hills and soup pots of Tuscany, the region is known as the land of the bean eaters. One variety in particular, the small, pale yellow Zolfino bean, is so special it's protected by DOP designation (Denominazione di Origine Protetta [Protected Designation of Origin]) because it grows best in poor soil with no irrigation at high elevations in specific areas of Arezzo.

But beans are prized all over Italy, from the Lamon beans grown near the peaks of the Dolomites in Veneto to the black chickpeas of Puglia's famed zuppa di ceci neri. And on tables all over the country, you'll find big, flat corona beans lavished in good olive oil, lemon, and herbs.

Clearly, there is a big world of beans beyond the usual supermarket varieties, each with wonderfully nuanced flavors and textures. Just remember: The fresher the beans, the better the results will be—they'll cook faster and more evenly and retain more flavor. Ideally, you want beans that are no older than a year since harvest. When you're ready to explore il mondo dei fagioli, Rancho Gordo, purveyor of high-quality heirloom beans, is a great place to start.

Homemade Ricotta

MAKES 5 CUPS

* - - ● ● ● ● ● ● ● - ● ● ● ● ● ● ● ● ● ● ● ● ● ● ● ● ● - ●

Ricotta means "recooked" in Italian, and it was so named because it was traditionally made from the whey leftover from making other cheeses. Italian frugality at its finest! These days, however, home cooks don't usually have leftover whey on hand, so fresh ricotta starts with milk and is cooked just once, resulting in a luxuriously creamy and soft fresh cheese that tastes heavenly when it's still fresh and warm. It's the closest you can get to farm-fresh ricotta (which is something you should never pass up if you ever get the chance to have it).

Fresh ricotta is dear to Italians, and it's at its cloudlike best on the day you make it. That's when you should showcase it on Bruschetta con Salsa di Pomodoro (page 6) or with a sweet preserve, such as Cantaloupe Confettura (page 191). It can even be served as a dessert with poached cherries or Piedmontese Baked Peaches (page 158) on top. The second day is when it goes into things you cook, such as pastas, whether stuffed into ravioli or swirled into a sauce. No matter which day you enjoy it, you'll find it's flavor is far superior to store-bought ricotta, which has been sitting around in cold storage for who knows how long.

There are just a few tips to ensure success. First, use regular lemons, not Meyer lemons, as you'll need the juice to be acidic enough to coagulate the milk. Second, resist the urge to stir after adding the juice. A little agitation of the milk is fine, but you want to avoid breaking up the curds into tiny particles. After straining, you'll be blessed with several cups of cloudy, golden whey that's rich in protein and really versatile. You could boil it again to make true ricotta (although it wouldn't make much), use it to marinate meats, or simply toss it into smoothies for an added protein boost.

1 gallon whole milk
1 cup heavy cream
1 heaping tablespoon flaky sea salt

½ cup plus 2 tablespoons strained freshly squeezed lemon juice (not Meyer lemon)

Set a colander over a large bowl and line it with a clean, damp floursack dish towel or three layers of damp cheesecloth.

Combine the milk, cream, and salt in a large, heavy-bottomed, nonreactive pot. Bring the mixture to 190°F over medium heat, testing frequently with a thermometer and gently

continues

stirring with a rubber spatula to keep the milk at the bottom of the pot from sticking. You'll see the milk starting to steam and bubbles beginning to form around the edges of the pot. Turn off the heat.

Slowly stir in ½ cup of the lemon juice. Once all the lemon juice has been added, stop stirring and wait a moment until you start to see curds forming. If the milk hasn't started to become translucent and thin-looking with curds starting to form, add another 1 or 2 tablespoons of lemon juice. Then, very slowly and gently, use the spatula to move the milk up from the bottom a few times to encourage even distribution without breaking up the curds too much as they form. Allow the mixture to rest for 15 minutes.

Gently ladle the curds into the prepared colander, letting the whey flow into the bowl below. Let the curds drain for 15 to 30 minutes (the longer they drain, the thicker the texture will be). At this point, the curds can be used right away as a spread on crostini or transferred to an airtight container and refrigerated for up to 1 week. For a thicker texture, allow the ricotta to keep draining overnight in the refrigerator. Refrigerate or freeze the whey and use in smoothies, soups, or marinades.

Cantaloupe Confettura

MAKES 3½ CUPS

Making jams and preserves doesn't have to be a big to-do resulting in dozens of jars for the pantry. Small-batch preserves destined for the fridge are just as rewarding and a lot less fuss. This recipe makes practical use of summer's plethora of perfumed muskmelons, such as cantaloupe, Charentais, crenshaw, and honeydew. It has a simple, honeylike flavor that's a wonderful accompaniment to cured meats and cheeses on a tagliere board.

1 large (2½- to 3-pound) ripe but not mushy cantaloupe or other muskmelon

1½ cups sugar

2 lemons

2 tablespoons Pernod (optional)

Cut the melon in half and scoop out the seeds. Cut each half into quarters, then run your knife between the peel and the flesh to remove the peel. Cut the melon into 2-inch chunks.

Combine the melon and sugar in a medium bowl, gently tossing to combine. Cover with plastic wrap and allow to macerate overnight in the refrigerator.

Use a vegetable peeler to remove the yellow zest from the lemons in wide strips, taking care to avoid the white pith. Slice crosswise into very thin strips. Cut the ends off the lemons to expose the flesh. Pare the white pith away from the lemons. Working over a bowl to catch the juices, cut between the membranes of the lemons to remove the segments. Cut the flesh into large pieces. Pick out and discard any seeds.

Transfer the melon mixture to a wide jam pot, nonreactive saucepan, or enameled Dutch oven. Add the lemon flesh and collected juice, zest, membranes, and cut ends (you'll remove these later) and bring to a boil over high heat. Lower the heat to a simmer and cook until the jam reaches 220°F, 20 to 30 minutes. Stir in the Pernod (if using). Use tongs to remove the membranes and lemon ends and discard.

Ladle the mixture into sterilized pint- or half-pint-size jars, wipe the rims, and seal with the lids. Turn the jars upside down and allow to cool before refrigerating (turning upside down helps the lids create a tight seal).

Rosé and Champagne Vinegar Cherries

MAKES 2 PINTS

I feel so lucky to have access to a wide variety of cherries in the Pacific Northwest, and I'm always looking for ways to preserve their flavor so I can enjoy them all year round. Giving them the quick pickle treatment is very easy and transforms them into a versatile and long-keeping pantry staple that's a fantastic accompaniment to cured meats and cheeses. They're even a great cocktail garnish. You can also put the brine to good use. It has a gorgeous ruby hue and a very shrublike flavor that's not overly sharp or too sweet, making it an ideal mixer for fizzy water, spritzes, and other cocktail creations that can use a tart cherry boost. I like to leave the pits inside so they can impart a subtle almond flavor as the cherries get infused with the brine.

1 pound Bing or Rainier cherries, stems removed

1 cup Champagne vinegar

1 cup rosé wine

⅔ cup sugar

¼ teaspoon fennel seeds

¼ teaspoon coriander seeds

Pinch of salt

Pack the cherries loosely in two clean, sterilized pint-size jars.

Combine the Champagne vinegar, wine, sugar, fennel seeds, coriander seeds, and salt in a small nonreactive saucepan. Set over medium-high heat and bring to a boil, stirring to dissolve the sugar. Lower the heat to medium-low and simmer for 5 minutes. Remove from the heat.

Pour the hot vinegar mixture over the cherries, taking care that the cherries are fully covered by the vinegar. Seal with lids and refrigerate. Leave in the refrigerator for at least 1 month before using to allow the flavors to meld fully.

ACKNOWLEDGMENTS

The circumference of my kitchen is almost completely lined with cookbooks, each one as beloved to me as an old friend. To finally add my own cookbook to the shelf—a little piece of my heart that might become someone else's friend in the kitchen, too—is a dream come true.

Although the journey from idea to printed page had no shortage of challenges, I was fortunate to have many wonderful people helping me along the way.

Huge thanks to my agent, Sharon Bowers, who believed in me from the very beginning and never gave up on getting my first book out in the world. My good friend Martha Holmberg was instrumental in lifting everything off the ground. And my cowriter, Danielle Centoni, wrangled all of my stories and recipes into a book people can read with pleasure and follow with success. I'm forever grateful to the immensely talented Kate Lewis for bringing everything to life with her gorgeous watercolor art.

A cookbook is only as good as its recipes, and I had an army of skilled cooks helping me ensure each and every one in this book is as delicious and fail-proof as possible. Shout-out to the Nostrana crew for always being ready and willing to pitch in and help: head baker Wren Busby, pastry chef Maddie Stratton, bartender Russell Smith, event chef Sara Woods, chef de cuisine Justin Carr, executive chef Bryan Donaldson, and former executive chef Brian Murphy. My chef friend Linda Colwell and baking ace Piper Davis provided much-appreciated assists, while cookbook author Faith Willinger has been hugely instrumental to my ongoing education in Italian cuisine over the years. And our cadre of recipe testers were invaluable in helping us work out every last kink: Helen Baldus, Jodie Chase, Lota LaMontagne, JoAnna Rodriguez, Vanessa Salvia, and Dakota Sloop.

I owe many thanks to Ann Treistman, editorial director of Countryman Press, for taking a chance on this sweet little ode to Italian summers and leading her talented team as they turned it into a book worth savoring: managing editor Jess Murphy, editorial assistant Maya Goldfarb, art director and designer Allison Chi, production manager Devon Zahn, copyeditor Iris Bass, proofreader Kathryn Flynn, compositors Ken Hansen and Tom Ernst, publicist Zachary Polendo, and marketing manager Devorah Backman.

Through it all, my assistant Andrew Dupuy has supplied unwavering patience and expert organization to keep things moving even when I was 6,000 miles away. And words can't begin to capture the gratitude I have for my partner, David West. With every leap of faith, he's always been right there with me.

INDEX

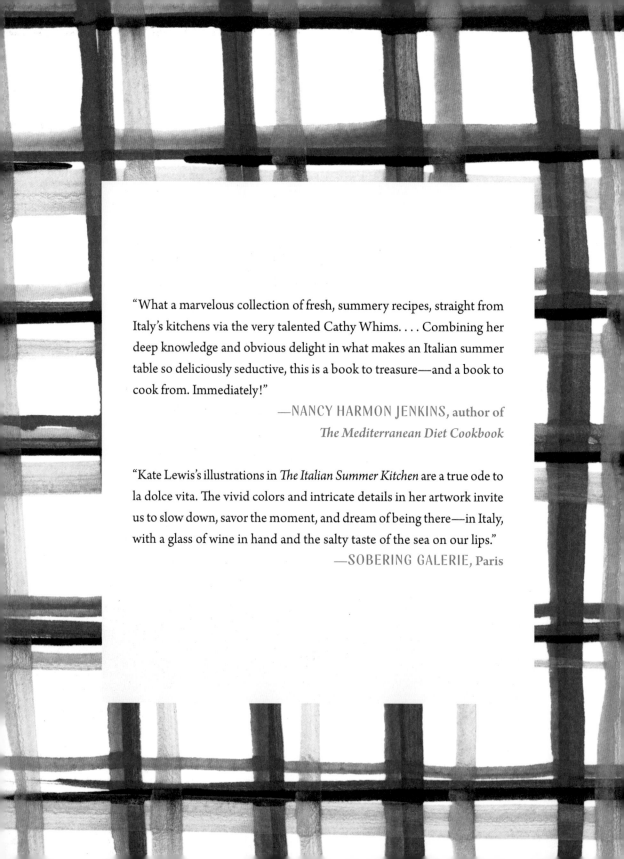

"What a marvelous collection of fresh, summery recipes, straight from Italy's kitchens via the very talented Cathy Whims. . . . Combining her deep knowledge and obvious delight in what makes an Italian summer table so deliciously seductive, this is a book to treasure—and a book to cook from. Immediately!"

—NANCY HARMON JENKINS, author of
The Mediterranean Diet Cookbook

"Kate Lewis's illustrations in *The Italian Summer Kitchen* are a true ode to la dolce vita. The vivid colors and intricate details in her artwork invite us to slow down, savor the moment, and dream of being there—in Italy, with a glass of wine in hand and the salty taste of the sea on our lips."

—SOBERING GALERIE, Paris